S0-CFD-753

#WHATIS

#WHATIS
POST-TRAUMATIC
GROWTH?

The Journey from Adversity to Growth

MIRIAM AKHTAR

This edition first published in the UK and USA 2017 by
Watkins, an imprint of Watkins Media Limited
19 Cecil Court
London WC2N 4EZ

enquiries@watkinspublishing.com

Design and typography copyright © Watkins Media Limited 2017

Text copyright © Miriam Akhtar 2017

Miriam Akhtar has asserted her right under the Copyright, Designs
and Patents Act 1988 to be identified as the author of this work.

All rights reserved.
No part of this book may be reproduced or utilized in any form
or by any means, electronic or mechanical,
without prior permission in writing from the Publishers.

1 3 5 7 9 10 8 6 4 2

Designed and typeset by Manisha Patel

Printed and bound in Germany

A CIP record for this book is available from the British Library

ISBN: 978-1-78028-979-3

www.watkinspublishing.com

CONTENTS

Why read this book?

Sometimes in life an event shakes us to the core. It could be a sudden death or the shock of a diagnosis of terminal illness. It could be something outside normal experience, like being caught in an earthquake, or a common but no less traumatic development such as a divorce. Such things have a huge impact, sending out shockwaves that can rock every corner of our world. They can leave us feeling lost, overwhelmed and vulnerable. The good news is that this doesn't have to define us. In fact it can herald a new beginning.

'Post-traumatic stress' (PTS) is something that we hear about a lot, for example among survivors of 9/11 and soldiers who served in Iraq and Afghanistan. The coverage has led to a growing awareness of the far-reaching effects of trauma and 'post-traumatic stress disorder', known as PTSD. This was first identified in military veterans (see page 42) but we are coming to understand that it is experienced more widely.

Although most of us will have to deal with extreme stresses at some point in life, these don't have to condemn us to eternal suffering. There can be a way ahead. If you have picked up this book because you think you, or someone you know, may be suffering from post-traumatic stress, I hope you will find it comforting to hear that something more positive may also be taking place: something that will allow us to experience positive change as a consequence of trauma. This is post-traumatic growth (PTG).

My intention in writing this book is to provide you with an introductory guide to trauma, PTS and PTG. We can't deny that traumatic experiences are both difficult and life-altering, but they can also be the catalyst for personal growth. My wish is to show that there can be a silver lining to trauma and that it can bring about a positive transformation.

20 reasons to start reading

1 Understand the nature of trauma.

2 Recognize the signs of post-traumatic stress (PTS).

3 Understand the difference between PTS and PTSD.

4 Discover the three major changes that happen with PTG.

5 Get to know the five dimensions of PTG.

6 Understand how PTG can change life for the better.

7 Learn from the stories of people who've experienced PTG.

8 Draw on modern science to support the healing process.

9 Understand the body–mind connection in trauma.

10 Practise self-care while going through extreme stress.

11 Strengthen your resilience to cope with challenges.

12 Use positive psychology to rebuild your well-being.

13 Be better equipped to support a loved one through trauma.

14 Understand how people grow through adversity.

15 Adopt a 'growth mindset' to lay the foundations for PTG.

16 Discover a new sense of meaning and purpose.

17 Explore five pathways to PTG.

18 Experience the deeper form of happiness known as 'eudaimonic well-being' (see pages 133–135).

19 Feel encouraged to embark on a fresh chapter in life.

20 Apply new knowledge to move from surviving toward thriving.

This book aims to point you to the tools that can help you reach the light at the end of the tunnel. It is possible to emerge stronger from the most testing of times and PTG can take you toward a life of greater meaning and deeper happiness.

Key features of this book

This book combines the science of PTG with real-life stories of people experiencing it. Apart from a few exceptions, all names have been changed to preserve the anonymity of the people who shared their stories.

In the Introduction I explain how I came to have an interest in post-traumatic growth through my work and my own personal experience. Chapter 1 explains the characteristics of trauma and how to recognize the symptoms of post-traumatic stress. Chapter 2 outlines the five key features of PTG and three ways in which it can change our lives. Chapter 3 focuses on the body and self-care while Chapter 4 looks at the mind and resilience. Finally Chapter 5 explores the transformative process of PTG and its impact on spiritual well-being.

The book is designed to make PTG as accessible as possible with the help of the following features:

- A Q&A approach that, chapter by chapter, explores the questions that are often asked about PTG.
- 'Case Study' boxes that share real-life experiences of PTG.
- 'Focus On' boxes that explore particular elements of PTG and therapies that can help achieve this.
- 'Try It' boxes that give you practical exercises to try out to help you on the road from adversity to growth.
- Finally, a 'What Next' section, including a further reading list, suggests how to continue your exploration of PTG.

KEY ABBREVIATIONS

The following abbreviations are used throughout the book for key terms:

PTG – Post-traumatic growth
PTS – Post-traumatic stress
PTSD – Post-traumatic stress disorder

INTRODUCTION

Why this subject?

Most of us will suffer trauma at some point in our lives. It's part of being human. When we do hit a major crisis, the extreme stress can shatter our emotional well-being and overwhelm our ability to cope. Trauma disrupts our lives, yet it used to be that people were expected to keep a lid on their emotions and just 'get on with it'. It was a taboo subject and people were often left in despair, silently tormented by distressing symptoms such as flashbacks which could go on for years.

This book intends to challenge those taboos about post-traumatic stress, making it clear that PTS is a normal, natural response to abnormal events. There's nothing to feel guilty or ashamed about.

Awareness of post-traumatic stress disorder has grown greatly, largely due to the increasing numbers being diagnosed with it. However, PTSD still tends to be associated with events outside normal experience, such as acts of war or terrorism. This very limited take on trauma urgently needs upgrading for the 21st century as it's not so much what happens that determines whether an event is traumatic, but our subjective emotional experience of it. The truth is that the more vulnerable and helpless we feel, the more likely we are to be traumatized by all kinds of unexpected negative events, whether that's being the victim of an assault, suffering a major financial loss or facing relentless stresses from working in a toxic environment. As we search for ways to deal with the crisis, we may question all aspects of our lives as we try to make sense of the adversity.

People sometimes find it hard to recognize that they are suffering from PTS and therefore often lack the tools to help themselves. The purpose of this book is to offer a way *through* trauma. There is an urgent need for a more positive approach to give people hope in the bleakest of times and the confidence that something good can emerge from the suffering. 'I no longer see what life took from me – I see what it gave me,' says Tara Lal, a firefighter, whose story is one of the case studies in this book.

Why me?

I first came across PTG during my training in positive psychology, which is the study of optimal human functioning – what it takes to feel good and function well. One of positive psychology's concepts is of people growing through adversity. This intrigued me as I had experienced this process myself. The trauma of losing my father when I was young shaped the course of my life. I learnt that life is short and that i had to apply myself to make the most of it. When you've been through the worst thing possible, nothing else ever seems as bad or as difficult to cope with.

The loss did, however, sow the seeds for later episodes of depression, and it was through the search for a solution that I discovered positive psychology. To my relief, I found the scientifically grounded tools that helped me develop a more sustainable happiness. I went on to become one of the first people in the UK to qualify as a positive psychologist, in 2009, gaining the MAPP – the MSc in Applied Positive Psychology. This course was established by Prof. Martin Seligman, the co-founder of the field, at the University of Pennsylvania, 'to make the world a happier place, parallel to the way clinical psychologists have made the world a less unhappy place.'

As soon as I qualified I began working with people to help them flourish in their personal and professional lives. And today I still work one-to-one as a coach as well as designing well-being programmes that range from Positive Youth to Positive Ageing, all work that I find hugely meaningful.

Mental health is one of my areas of expertise and in 2012 I wrote the book *Positive Psychology for Overcoming Depression*, which was a ground-breaking departure from the traditional approach to depression. The book has now been published around the world and I love hearing from readers who have been helped by it. It's made me aware of how useful self-help books can be to sustain people through their dark night of the soul.

Life sometimes throws a curveball at you and a few years ago, in the space of one month, I suffered a double trauma. Out of the blue I became the target of a very modern crime – cyberstalking – and hard on its heels came another experience, which brought back all the distress of my childhood loss. My mother collapsed and was taken into intensive care at the hospital where my father had died. I was at a conference in Amsterdam and my emergency flight home was delayed. I paced around the airport, desperate to get to my mother's bedside in time. When I got to the hospital I found myself walking down the very corridor where 40 years earlier I had witnessed my father's face contorting as his heart arrested. I was taken into a private room where a doctor told me that my mother had less than a 40 per cent chance of survival. One of these crises might have severely tested my resilience, but having two to deal with crushed me. After months of turmoil I was eventually diagnosed with PTSD.

My turning point came on the day I was confiding in a friend about the cyberstalking. She looked at me and said: 'Miriam, you can do something with this. You can use this experience to help others in the future.' And that's how I began to shift out of the grip of fear and into a place of motivation. I realized that I could help myself and others going through a similar experience. My journalistic skills resurfaced and I began to explore the practices that you'll find in this book.

At the core of this book are techniques that build resilience. I train frontline medics in resilience skills and have facilitated one of the major courses in the field, the Penn Resilience Programme. Originally developed at the University of Pennsylvania to support adolescent well-being, it is now being delivered at an adult level across the American military, from where a lot of the research on PTG has emerged.

I have given talks on resilience at various conferences and healthcare facilities including the Bristol Cancer Help Centre, now known as Penny Brohn UK, a charity that is a pioneer of complementary cancer care. I've seen people after the trauma of their cancer diagnosis expressing a desperate need for ways to help themselves. I have also had the privilege of seeing how people go on to grow despite dealing with life-threatening illness. They know what's important and who's important to them.

There's no doubt that trauma can be an enfeebling experience when you're in the thick of it, yet I now feel stronger than I did before. My hope is that this book will help to strengthen you too.

Why now?

The concept of growing through adversity is not a new one. 'That which does not kill us makes us stronger' is a well-known saying attributed to the philosopher Friedrich Nietzsche. The phoenix rising from the ashes is a long-established symbol of rebirth that is highly relevant to PTG. At the end of the phoenix's long life its nest catches fire and burns ferociously, reducing the bird to ashes. But out of those ashes a young phoenix emerges – renewed and stronger than before: the perfect symbol of regeneration after a life-altering event.

Many ancient forms of spirituality, including Christianity, Buddhism and Judaism, speak of the transformative power of suffering. What is new is that there is now a *science* of PTG. Studies by the Posttraumatic Growth Research Group at the University of North Carolina, the Post-Traumatic Growth Unit at the University of East London and the Centre for Trauma, Resilience and Growth at the University of Nottingham have all confirmed that people can and do experience benefits from adversity.

With mental health disorders on the rise in our fast-moving, increasingly pressured world, there is a grave need for greater choice in treatment methods. As help is often hard to access through health services or expensive to fund yourself, the knowledge in this book gives you self-help tools to cope positively in stressful circumstances, stand firm while the storm rages around you and make the longed-for journey toward a renewed and flourishing life.

CHAPTER 1
What is trauma? And what is post-traumatic stress?

Experiencing the dark side of life, such as the sudden death of a loved one, the shock of a diagnosis of illness or the end of a significant relationship, are all normal parts of being human. If we look back over the generations of our parents and grandparents, there are many examples of hardship and horrors, everything from deprivation to war. Trauma is an experience of the brain and body in reaction to conditions of great stress. Mostly we do find the courage and strength to adapt to events that take us to our limits. The spirit is surprisingly hardy and can recover from testing experiences.

How do we experience stress?

The stress response is at the core of a traumatic experience. Stress is the body's way of responding to any kind of demand and reacting to what it perceives as threatening situations – whether those are real or imagined. In physiological terms stress releases hormones that prepare us for 'fight or flight', gearing us up to take action. Feeling 'stressed' has come to be a defining feature of modern life, whether that is dealing with job insecurity or juggling work/life balance. While we tend to think of stress as generally a negative thing, it does have an upside. A little stress can motivate us to get started on a project and a deadline can help sharpen our focus.

Being exposed to stressful situations on an intermittent basis can even serve to strengthen us so that we're better

FOCUS ON THE 'FIGHT OR FLIGHT' RESPONSE

The autonomic nervous system, which regulates our internal organs, has two main branches:

- The parasympathetic nervous system (PNS) – the branch that helps us to 'rest and digest', taking us into a state of calm and relaxation.
- The sympathetic nervous system (SNS) – the branch that produces the stress response, aka 'fight or flight', which primes the body to defend itself against threat, an essential part of our survival mechanism.

When the SNS is in control, stress hormones such as cortisol and adrenaline are released, the heart rate increases, blood pressure rises, breathing accelerates and muscles tighten, ready for action. Traumatic stress is associated with being in constant 'fight or flight' mode – or its cousin the 'freeze', when we switch off and become numb in response to overwhelming events. A heightened state of the SNS, known as 'hyper-arousal', is an indicator that the body and mind have not yet recognized when a traumatic event is over. This state of increased psychological and physiological tension is one of the main symptoms of PTSD.

prepared for future stressors, like a form of 'stress inoculation'. However, prolonged stress, when life is continuously out of balance, can compromise our psychological, emotional and physical well-being. The question is, therefore, where does stress cross the line into something else? And at what point does stress turn into trauma?

How do people respond to major stress?

When people are faced with an extremely stressful event, there are three main ways in which they may respond. To use a real-life example, as I write this, floods have struck the south-west of England, close to where I live. In rural Somerset villages are under water and homes are drowning in thick, smelly mud. Roads have become rivers, communities are cut off from the outside world and businesses are in danger of collapse. When an emergency such as this happens, people may experience:

- A sense of being overwhelmed and traumatized with a lasting effect of it overshadowing their lives.
- Stress and strain for a time but then go on to make a recovery back to how they were before.
- A sense of positive change as a consequence of going through the adversity with surprising bonuses such as stronger friendships and community spirit, with people pulling together and looking out for each other.

The lesson in this is that it is not the event in itself that creates a 'trauma' but rather people's perception of what has happened to them. This is important because, as we'll find out later, only one person can say whether an experience was traumatic, and that is the individual going through it.

What is really meant by 'trauma'?

'Trauma' is a word that comes from the Greek for 'wound' and in the medical sense refers to a physical injury. In psychology it's a term used to describe highly distressing events that have the power to overwhelm. Traumatic experiences are often unexpected and uncontrollable occurrences that people feel unprepared for and powerless to prevent. They provoke intense fear, horror and a feeling of helplessness. Trauma poses a significant threat to our psychological and physical well-being. It often involves life-and-death scenarios that happen to us or that we witness in others. A traumatizing experience shakes the foundations of our beliefs about safety and shatters our trust in life. It causes emotional, psychological and physical harm, which can seriously disrupt the course of our lives.

How do you know when you're experiencing trauma?

Historically, and often still today, we tend to think of traumatic events as horrendous one-off incidents, like being the victim of an assault or caught up in an act of terrorism, but they

CASESTUDY SURVIVING A TSUNAMI

This trauma survivor was caught up in the 2004 Indian Ocean tsunami. 'My partner and I were on a beautiful beach in Thailand when the tsunami struck. Having stepped inside a bamboo hut just seconds before, I quickly, and terrifyingly, became submerged as the water crashed in. I was thrown around underwater like a ragdoll and smashed several times against the back wall, but then somehow I surfaced outside the hut, presumably after a second wave had knocked down some of the walls. I then swam as hard as I could but I was being pulled out to sea when a Thai man appeared in a tree and somehow – to this day I still don't know how – managed to pull me into it, to safety.

It was only later after we swam to dry land that I was lucky enough to find my partner, who had been separated from me in the chaos. He was in a bad way by this stage due to his injuries. Several days later we made it to a hospital in Bangkok, where his head wound was addressed and his leg was saved.'

Find out how our trauma survivor coped in the aftermath of the tsunami on page 29.

can also involve lower-level repeated incidents. This book is using a wider definition of trauma to include chronic, insidious experiences such as the coercive control involved in abusive relationships, where the relentlessness and stress of the situation can trigger a traumatic reaction. The circumstances may include a betrayal of trust, abuse of power, pain, confusion, entrapment, loss or other negative experiences.

What makes something a traumatic experience?

Whether someone is traumatized by what has happened will depend on a wide range of circumstances including their:

CASESTUDY **AUTHOR IS CYBERSTALKED**

'One day out of the blue I was contacted by a client, who was perplexed by a malicious email they'd received about me. I was shocked and embarrassed. As I looked into it I discovered that the culprit was posting lies online while at the same time trying to impersonate my business. I felt wave after wave of horror as I uncovered the scale of his campaign of cyber harassment. It was the obsessiveness of it that was most frightening. It was like he was trying to destroy me and I felt powerless to stop him.'

- **subjective experience** of the event – e.g. when someone in an accident *believes* they are going to die.
- **personal circumstances,** including any other pressures they are under and if they have recently suffered other traumas.
- **physical health,** whether they're in good health or more vulnerable as a result of illness.
- **mental health,** including coping skills and resilience levels.
- **support** that they have around them at the time of the incident.

No two people's experience will ever be the same. Whether it is a one-off incident that leaves you in a state of helplessness and hopelessness or the reaction to a prolonged stress that eats away at your resilience, it's up to you to decide if it has been a traumatic experience.

What kind of experiences can trigger a trauma?

In the list below I've included some of the more common events that can lead to a traumatic reaction as well as a broad range of others. However, it's important to remember that absolutely any distressing occurrence or situation has the potential to be traumatic, whether you experienced it directly or witnessed it.

- Accidents
- Bullying
- Child abuse or neglect
- Crime

- Cyber harassment
- Death, especially a sudden death or suicide
- Discrimination
- Divorce
- Domestic violence
- Emotional abuse
- Entrapment
- Financial crisis or loss
- Harassment
- Homelessness
- Incarceration
- Maltreatment or neglect
- Man-made disasters e.g. chemical spills, nuclear accidents
- Military combat and service
- Natural disasters e.g. floods, earthquakes, volcanic eruptions
- Racism
- Rape
- Relationship breakdown
- Scapegoating or shunning
- Serious illness
- Sexual abuse or assault
- Stalking
- Surgery
- Terrorism
- Toxic workplaces
- Traumatic birth
- Traumatic separation

This list doesn't cover every possibility so I recommend also taking a look at the symptoms that are listed on pages 30–33 to help you evaluate your own particular experience and identify whether or not you've been suffering from post-traumatic stress.

People react in very different ways to trauma, making it hard to predict how symptoms will manifest and across what timeframe. Shock, denial and emotional numbing are common immediately after a horrific incident as people find it hard to comprehend and adjust to the new reality. The reaction can come in waves and reappear after a period of absence. A trauma can also catch you by surprise by revisiting you at later points in life, in particular at times when you are vulnerable for other reasons. Trauma often involves a sense of loss, whether of a loved one, the life you were living, a job, home or relationship and, at a fundamental level, it represents a loss of your sense of safety in life. As such, it is normal to go through a grieving process following the traumatic event.

What is post-traumatic stress (PTS)?

PTS is a normal stress reaction that follows on from a traumatic event, which appears as any of a wide range of emotional, behavioural, physical and social symptoms (see the lists on pages 30–33) that occur as the mind slips into a state of overwhelm and the body into fight, flight or freeze mode. The key to understanding PTS is recognizing that what is going on is a natural, and indeed helpful, response to what is perceived as a dangerous situation.

In my own experience of PTS, one of the most difficult aspects was the insomnia. I'd pace around at night and go to the window to check and see if my cyberstalker was there. My face was red and raw, covered in patches of eczema.

I couldn't concentrate and was in such a state that I was unable to work. I stopped going out at night and would get panicky about going up to London to see clients. Some of my fillings fell out because I was grinding my teeth. I felt like I was imploding, swinging between periods of high anxiety and then feeling so low that I was barely able to function.

CASESTUDY **AFTER THE TSUNAMI**

The journey to recovery was not straightforward for the tsunami survivor we met on page 24. 'It was the body and mind's amazing instinct for survival which got me through early on. Back in the UK, my partner suffered badly from depression while I, on the other hand, felt strong, feeling lucky just to be alive and to have the support of so many friends and family. However, about a year later, as he was starting to recover, I began to feel disproportionately overwhelmed by things and then, one day, I couldn't get out of bed. My back had gone and I just lay there crying, not really knowing why. I found it hard to function on a day-to-day level, as everything felt so heavy and difficult. I was checked over by various specialists, and the consensus was that I was suffering from classic PTS symptoms.'

How do you recognize the signs of PTS or PTSD?

Although trauma is a unique experience for each individual, there are common features to traumatic stress. Whether you are suffering from PTS or the more extreme PTSD, it is likely that you will relate to some of the physical, emotional, behavioural and social symptoms described in the lists that follow, which have been sourced primarily from mental health and medical guides including MIND, HelpGuide and Web-MD (please see the Further Reading and Useful Websites sections, pages 138–141, for details of these and others). In real life there is considerable overlap between the symptoms of PTS, which is a normal stress reaction, and PTSD, which is considered to be a medical disorder. For that reason I've made the list inclusive of both. There are, however, particular criteria for a diagnosis of PTSD (see pages 35–37).

Physical symptoms

Let's start with the physical symptoms of trauma. The body is in a state of heightened physiological stress, signs of which include being easily startled and finding it hard to fall asleep. You may also feel extremely tired due to sleep disturbances and peaks and troughs of stress hormones like adrenaline and cortisol. Physical symptoms include the following:

- Racing heart
- Muscle tension
- Excessive startle response
- Shaky hands

- Insomnia
- Bad dreams
- Fatigue
- Headaches
- Lowered immune functioning
- Digestive upsets and problems
- Aches and pains
- Loss of appetite
- Lower libido

Emotional symptoms

A feeling of helplessness and hopelessness are both common features of PTS, as are a variety of negative emotions, from being held in the grip of fear to feeling weighed down with sadness. 'Survivor's guilt' is another common experience for victims of incidents in which others have died. Often people swing between highs and lows. Positive emotions are largely absent, although this is not a black and white scenario. It is entirely possible and indeed human to experience both positive and negative emotions at the same time – moments of joy tinged with sadness, for example.

Behavioural symptoms

A trauma can impact on how well you function and your behaviour in everyday life. Hypervigilance is common in PTS, repeatedly scanning your environment for anything that feels threatening or may be linked to the trauma. This can lead to some obsessive behaviour patterns. Behavioural PTS symptoms include:

- Extreme alertness, on the lookout for signs of danger
- Agitation
- Avoidance of places associated with the trauma
- Confusion and disorientation
- Detachment
- Disassociation
- Disbelief and denial of the events
- Poor concentration
- Intrusive thoughts and memories
- Difficulty with decision-making
- Memory problems
- Loss of confidence and self-esteem
- Loss of interest in usual activities
- Self-blame

Social symptoms

As well as wrecking our inner world, the ripples of trauma often disrupt our relationships, damage how we interact with others in daily life, and undermine our trust in the world. So look out for signs such as:

- A sense of alienation, rejection or abandonment
- Major conflict in relationships
- Blaming and distrust of others
- Vulnerability around people
- Social withdrawal and isolation

- Lower performance at work
- Overprotectiveness
- Reduced satisfaction with the world

PTS triggers

It's very common to have an acute stress reaction following a traumatic experience but PTS symptoms will usually subside as the trauma is processed.

However, even when recovered, it is possible to be troubled from time to time by painful memories or emotions, and for these to be triggered via the senses. Shooting survivors, for example, are often set off by sounds that resemble gunfire. 'The thing that gets me tearful is bottles of champagne popping. Balloons and fireworks are a big fear, and party poppers. I really don't like those,' says Aimie Adam, who, as a child, survived the 1996 Dunblane school massacre.

A female client of mine, who was a victim of sexual abuse, is triggered by seeing a certain make of car which was driven by the perpetrator. Her other senses can provoke a similar reaction too: 'Smelling a certain aftershave also makes me collapse for a few seconds. I just wake up on the floor.' Anniversaries, certain places or situations or even news items related to your trauma can be the triggers that plunge you straight back into full-scale distress.

Usually, with time and self-care, the symptoms of PTS will improve, but if they worsen or continue for months and interfere with your functioning, then it is important to see your doctor or another health professional with expertise in the area as there is a possibility that you may be suffering from the more serious post-traumatic stress disorder (PTSD).

What is PTSD?

It may surprise you to learn that the most common outcome following high adversity is NOT post-traumatic stress disorder (PTSD) but rather resilience, returning to your previous level of functioning after a short period of suffering. PTSD, on the other hand, is a complex and debilitating psychiatric disorder, in which symptoms such as flashbacks can persist for months and years after the adversity. Similarly PTSD symptoms can also emerge a long time after the traumatizing event.

The American Psychiatric Association classifies PTSD as a trauma- and stress-related disorder that can arise from exposure to actual or threatened death, serious injury or sexual violation. Their criteria for a diagnosis of PTSD are specific. The exposure is as a result of one of the following scenarios:

- Directly experiencing the traumatic event
- Witnessing the traumatic event in person

- Learning that the traumatic event occurred to a close family member or good friend (with the actual or threatened death being either violent or accidental)
- Experiencing first-hand repeated or extreme exposure to aversive details of the traumatic event

How is PTSD diagnosed?

PTSD is usually diagnosed when, more than a month after the traumatic event, symptoms are continuing to cause significant distress or disturbance, interfering with home, work, relationships or other important areas of functioning. According to the *Diagnostic and Statistical Manual of Mental Disorders* (*DSM-5*; the standard classification used by mental health professionals in the USA), an individual will have symptoms from each of four clusters for a diagnosis of PTSD:

- **Re-experiencing the trauma.** Flashbacks, memories or dreams, as well as intense distress in response to cues that represent some aspect of the traumatic event.
- **Hyperarousal.** A state of heightened physiological and psychological stress which can result in anxiety, fatigue and reduced tolerance to pain. An exaggerated startle response is a classic sign of hyperarousal, as is insomnia. It also often causes problems with concentration as well as anger, aggression, agitation, impulsiveness, irritability and reckless and self-destructive behaviour.

- **Avoidance of anything associated with the trauma.** This includes efforts to avoid memories, thoughts and feelings as well as external reminders – people, places, activities and situations that are linked to the event.
- **Negative alterations in thinking and mood.** Persistent and exaggerated negative thoughts, beliefs and emotions toward yourself and others, e.g. blaming yourself for what happened and feeling incapable of experiencing positive emotions.

There is also a dissociative subtype of PTSD. Someone experiencing this is likely to feel entirely detached from their life, as if:

- they are an outside observer of their own mind and body
- they or their world is not real
- they are in a dreamlike state

Women are more than twice as likely as men to develop post-traumatic stress disorder, according to the National Center for PTSD in the USA. It's suggested that around 10 per cent of women in the USA will experience PTSD at some point in their lives compared to 4 per cent of men. Amongst the emergency services, 20 per cent of firefighters are estimated to experience PTSD. The incidence is also high amongst military personnel, estimated at 11–20 per cent of veterans.

There are some gender differences in the experience of PTSD. Sexual assault and abuse are the major causes in women, whereas in men there are more diverse causes including accidents, physical assault, combat and disasters, and indirect causes such as witnessing death or injury. Depression, substance abuse and anxiety disorders frequently co-occur with PTSD. Women tend to experience 'internalizing' disorders such as depression and anxiety whereas with men it often

FOCUS ON UNDERSTANDING PTSD FLASHBACKS

Some experts prefer to think of PTSD as a psychological injury rather than a mental disorder. The brain suffers what is in essence a 'memory-filing error' when trying to process the trauma. This can be very distressing as the brain is unable to recognize the event as a normal 'memory' because it wasn't processed as one. All the elements of the trauma – the event itself, the emotions involved, together with sensations such as sights, sounds and smells – can end up being presented in the form of flashbacks, as if they are happening again. Such flashbacks cause an individual to be sent straight back into their trauma and feel as if they are re-experiencing it in the here and now.

manifests in externalizing symptoms such as rage, aggressive behaviour and substance misuse.

People most at risk of PTSD include those who have been exposed to life-and-death scenarios as witnesses, rescuers or supporters, or the perpetrators themselves. Trauma impacts on a wide range of first responders and other personnel who assist trauma survivors, such as social workers, therapists, health professionals and clergy. This is known as vicarious traumatization.

Are PTS and PTSD the same thing?

In everyday language PTS and PTSD are terms that are used interchangeably, although as we have seen there are specific criteria for a clinical diagnosis of PTSD. Many of the symptoms in PTSD are similar to PTS but the difference lies in the duration and intensity of symptoms. Dr Matthew Friedman, senior advisor to the American National Center for PTSD, likens it to the difference between a cold and pneumonia. They share many symptoms, but if your cold is extremely severe and hasn't gone away in more than a week, something more is at work and you should get it checked out. I find it helpful to think of a continuum with PTS at the milder end where the body and mind eventually succeed in consigning the trauma to the past. At the other end is the medical disorder of PTSD where problems processing the trauma mean that it continues to haunt the survivor in the present, and professional support should be sought.

Unfortunately many people suffer in silence, whether out of a sense of shame or simply not knowing what to do, which

---

FOCUSON **DIFFERENCES BETWEEN PTS AND PTSD**

PTS	PTSD
A traumatic experience that overwhelms the sufferer's ability to cope for a finite time	Experiencing or witnessing a life-threatening event that causes significant distress and disturbance
A normal stress response to a trauma	Clinically diagnosed psychiatric disorder
Symptoms usually last less than one month	Symptoms continue for more than one month or emerge later
Symptoms are intense at first but eventually subside	Symptoms are severe, persistent and can reoccur
Temporarily interferes with daily life	Has a significant and lasting impact on functioning

---

means that they can end up falling between the cracks, neither recognizing what is ailing them nor getting access to help. There is one clear advantage of being given a professional diagnosis of PTSD and that is that it opens up a potential pathway to treatment.

What is the history of PTSD?

Humans have always been exposed to trauma but in the past the symptoms that ensued were often put down to a weakness of character or body rather than a wound to the psyche. As early as the 17th century Swiss military physicians identified a condition they named 'nostalgia', which was characterized by melancholy, incessant thinking about home, disturbed sleep, loss of appetite, anxiety and cardiac palpitations. Other nationalities began to recognize the symptoms. The Germans called it *heimweh* or homesickness, while French doctors similarly named it *maladie du pays* and the Spanish *estar roto* – to be broken. This was a condition most often observed in soldiers but in civilian life there were also signs of the symptoms which would come to be associated with PTSD.

It was through the experience of war that PTSD eventually came to be identified but it took a long time to recognize that injuries sustained in war were psychological as well as physical. In the early 20th century, soldiers returning from the

CASESTUDY CHARLES DICKENS, A PTSD VICTIM?

In 1865 the novelist Charles Dickens had a brush with death when he was a passenger on a train which plunged off a viaduct into a river below. It took several hours for rescuers to arrive so Dickens worked amongst the dead and dying, witnessing trauma as well as suffering it himself. He later wrote about feeling 'curiously weak . . . and very nervous'. Dickens subsequently avoided travelling by train, finding it 'inexpressibly distressing'. At the time, rail accident victims without apparent physical wounds were found to be experiencing debilitating nerve problems such as trembling, exhaustion and chronic pain. This condition became known as 'railway spine' and was formally named 'Erichsen's disease' after the physician John Eric Erichsen, who described it in his 1866 publication: *On Railway and Other Injuries of the Nervous System*. Symptoms included memory impairment, poor concentration, sleep disturbance, anxiety, irritability, back stiffness and pain, hearing problems, numbness of extremities and head, hand and arm pain. Dickens's output dwindled after the crash and, in a strange coincidence, he died on its fifth anniversary. Maybe he was suffering from what we now know to be PTSD.

battlefields of World War One were observed suffering major anxiety, panic, agitation, helplessness, extreme sensitivity to noise and other symptoms of what we now know as PTSD. It was named 'shell shock' and thought to be caused by the impact on the brain of artillery shell explosions. Tragically this condition was little understood and sufferers were sometimes put on trial, and even executed, for military crimes such as desertion and cowardice.

Thinking began to change when soldiers who had not been in the line of fire were also found to be suffering from symptoms. Men were breaking down, unable to cope with the stresses of warfare. An inability to eat or sleep was common. A German doctor called Honigman came up with 'war neurosis' as a term to describe the multitude of nervous and mental disorders associated with military combat. Sigmund Freud, the founder of psychoanalysis, became involved in the diagnosis and treatment of this 'war neurosis'.

Through the course of subsequent wars the understanding of the condition evolved. The plight of American veterans of the Vietnam War, together with an emerging field of study on trauma, was the turning point that led to the modern definition of PTSD. In 1980 it made its first appearance in the third edition of the *Diagnostic and Statistical Manual*. The term 'post-traumatic stress disorder' (PTSD) was chosen to reflect the fact that the condition isn't only a phenomenon of war but had also been observed in victims of the Nazi Holocaust, the atomic bombings of Hiroshima and Nagasaki, and other traumas including torture, rape, natural disasters such as earthquakes, and man-made disasters such as factory explosions. The crucial change was the stipulation that the cause of PTSD lay outside the individual – it was a result of a traumatic event rather than an inherent personal weakness.

The criteria for a diagnosis of PTSD have broadened across subsequent editions of the *DSM*. The International Classification of Diseases (ICD) developed by the World Health Organization states that the PTSD patient 'must have been exposed to a stressful event or situation (either short or long-lasting) of an exceptionally threatening or catastrophic nature, which would be likely to cause pervasive distress in almost anyone'.

In summary

As we have seen in this chapter there is a lot of overlap between PTS and PTSD. I hope you'll find it reassuring to know that PTS is considered a natural and normal reaction to 'abnormal' events and that PTSD, while enormously distressing and debilitating at the time, can be the very thing that can act as the catalyst for post-traumatic growth (PTG), as we'll see in the next chapter.

CHAPTER 2

What is meant by
post-traumatic growth?

Post-traumatic growth (PTG) is the positive change that can happen in the wake of a traumatic event. When people go through trauma, alongside the distress they feel, they often discover something they value about themselves and change in ways that can add up to a personal transformation. PTG is the positive psychological change that comes about as a result of the struggle with highly challenging life circumstances. When we go through major adversity it is normal to fear that it will break us but in time people generally return to their previous level of well-being. PTG goes beyond recovery to something more positive emerging from the negative experience. Not simply a return

FOCUS ON EXAMPLES OF PTG

'I question everything now. Is this the type of work I'm supposed to be doing? There's so many things to question.'

'I see it as a second chance for life. My husband and I are adopting.'

These are the words of survivors of the plane that crash-landed on the Hudson River in New York in 2009. They are also examples of post-traumatic growth.

to baseline after a period of suffering, it is an experience of improved functioning. Research suggests that a traumatic event doesn't have to doom us to eternal suffering, instead it can act as a springboard to a life of higher well-being and deeper meaning. People who've experienced PTG talk about feeling stronger and having gained unexpected benefits from the adversity. This personal growth, many examples of which feature in this book, often marks a genuine turning point in their lives.

In what ways does PTG change your life?

Post-traumatic growth is both a process of transformation and a potential outcome after a period of grave adversity. There are three major areas of life in which people experience change:

1. Change in the self. Rising to the challenge of getting through the crisis reveals abilities in ourselves; this alters our self-perception. People grow in strength and wisdom and become more accepting of their vulnerabilities. This stronger self helps to protect them from future stresses.

2. Change in relationships. People experience a greater need for connection, feel closer to their loved ones, value their friends and family more, and have more compassion toward others.

CASESTUDY PTG AFTER CANCER

A publisher was diagnosed with cancer after finding a lump in her breast. Then her partner also received a cancer diagnosis. 'When the consultant told me: "You have breast cancer, we think it is stage 2," I was running a small business and we agreed that I would continue to work for as long as I felt able to. Along with the fear of dying of cancer, the interesting thing was that I also felt immense relief. "I can let go now." I had been feeling burdened by the business for some time but didn't want to let people down. The cancer became my friend in that curious way – it gave me a good reason to stop. Now Andrew and I have both finished our treatments and are well.

'Cancer brought about a profound change. It pushed me off my feeling that in order to be loved, to be a good person,

3. Change in philosophy of life. The impact of adversity leads to shifts in priorities and worldview. People re-evaluate what is important to them and have a greater appreciation of life.

I hope the publisher's story above will convince you that there can be a silver lining even in life's most difficult experiences – and that with adversity can also come a sense

I needed to be perfect and shiny and well. Instead I found that my body and brain were fallible and the world didn't fall apart. People still loved me. I let go of the business and it was OK. And I feel much more in touch with life – knowledge of my own vulnerability has helped me to open to others.

'There were many positives, to the extent that if you offered me the opportunity to change my history and not have cancer, I would not take you up on it. It made me see what was important. It made me cherish my wonderful network of friends and family and community. It made both Andrew and I realize that we needed to get on with our lives and do what we wanted, now, rather than in the future. It has brought us closer. We are walking 690 miles of the pilgrimage route to Santiago de Compostela in Spain and then we plan further travels. As he said to me the other day, "You know, life feels like an adventure again."'

of expansion and transformation. PTG doesn't in any way imply an absence of distress, or being in denial of the impact of trauma. It's simply that we know now there are ways to work through these tough times to achieve growth.

The relationship between trauma and growth is not straightforward. As you may expect, sometimes the severity of the trauma, such as in the case of a genocide, can be so huge that people may never fully recover. And at the other end of the scale, in more minor, short-lived incidents, there may not be quite enough adversity to lead to the 'struggle' which induces growth. According to one of the leading experts in the field, Prof. Stephen Joseph from the University of Nottingham, the most growth is likely to occur in those who are psychologically shaken by the trauma and experiencing some degree of PTS. This might even help us view PTS in a fresh light as the engine that drives the development of PTG.

The good news is that PTG is not only common but, in fact, outnumbers reports of PTSD. It's important to mention that PTG is not universal and there is no guarantee of it. However, recognizing that suffering and growth, or personal distress and personal development, can and do co-occur raises, in itself, the likelihood of it.

If you've been through something deeply traumatic, it's probably best to have no *expectation* of PTG but simply to be receptive to the possibility of it. I've come across many cases of PTG through my work, sometimes occurring decades after the original trauma. This was the case for firefighter Tara Lal, who suffered a double tragedy in childhood with her mother's death followed by her brother's suicide (see pages 54–55).

Where did the concept of PTG come from?

The phenomenon of positive change as a result of adversity has been documented throughout history by philosophers and theologians. All the major religious traditions have something to say about how we respond to suffering but it wasn't until the 1990s that psychologists established a field of research exploring the concept of growth through adversity. The term 'post-traumatic growth' was coined by psychologists Richard Tedeschi and Lawrence Calhoun at the University of North Carolina in the mid-1990s. It is also sometimes known in psychology circles as 'adversarial growth', 'psychological growth', 'benefit finding', 'stress-related growth' and 'perceived benefits'.

The events of 9/11 significantly heightened interest in PTG. The terrorist attacks of 2001 shocked the USA to the core and left a mark on the American psyche. Yet, even in the first few months of national trauma, there were reports of positive changes. A rise in altruistic behaviour, for instance, with people coming forward to donate blood, time or money to help the survivors and bereaved.

What kind of traumatic experiences lead to PTG?

British psychologists Alex Linley and Stephen Joseph carried out one of the first reviews of PTG studies in 2004, with PTG being reported across a wide range of adversities, including:

- **Transport accidents** such as shipping disasters, car crashes, aviation incidents. See the case study of PTG after an accident on pages 124–125.
- **Natural disasters** such as hurricanes, earthquakes.
- **Interpersonal assaults** e.g. combat, sexual violence, child abuse.
- **Illnesses** such as cancer (see case study of the cancer survivor on pages 48–49), heart attacks, leukaemia, rheumatoid arthritis, multiple sclerosis, HIV/AIDS.
- **Life events** e.g. relationship breakdown, parental divorce, bereavement, emigration. See the case study on financial loss on the opposite page.

What are the main benefits of PTG?

As already mentioned, PTG leads to major change in our sense of self, relationships and life philosophy/priorities, but what about the ways in which it can benefit our lives? Richard Tedeschi and Lawrence Calhoun have mapped, in their 'transformational model' of PTG, five key areas in which growth occurs:

- **Personal strength**
- **Closer relationships**
- **Greater appreciation for life**
- **New possibilities**
- **Spiritual development**

CASESTUDY FINDING STRENGTH
AFTER FINANCIAL LOSS

A trainee osteopath from Iceland and her family lost
their homes to the country's bankruptcy in 2008.

'The sudden reality was that we had virtually nothing
left. My new home was taken by the bank for almost
nothing. I remember once I hardly had money for food
but I didn't tell anyone because most of the people
closest to me had left Iceland. It was very hard to see
my family give up and move abroad to start again.

'I have been through a lot in my life but the experience
of losing everything financially and seeing my family
go through the same has only made me stronger and
more focused on what matters. Now I look back and
think how the experience simplified my life. What I have
realized is that what matters is love and that never goes
away and sometimes is only discovered by peeling
all the material stuff away. I look at my son and simply
appreciate that we have food to eat and smiles on
our faces. I feel stronger and view the experience as a
test of my strength. Counting crabs with my son on the
beach is more important than counting pennies.'

CASESTUDY A FIREFIGHTER'S STORY

'As a young girl, I felt lost, isolated and confused by grief as
a result of the death of my mother, so I clung to my elder
brother. He became my rock when everything else in my
life had given way beneath me. When I was 17 he took his
own life. My fragile world shattered around me and I found
myself engulfed in a tidal wave of grief.

'For many years I tried to put it to one side. It was only in my
thirties that the pain of my childhood started to play itself out
in my life when, as a firefighter, I attended a call to a suicide
followed by a colleague attempting suicide. With the help of
a psychologist I actively turned toward all the fear. Digging
into my past and reliving the grief as an adult made me
question life and, in amongst the darkness of grief, I found
beauty and wonder in the simplest of things and in doing so
found myself, my passions and my strength.

'Ever so slowly a transformation occurred within me.
I realized that the scars I held had given me the gift of
compassion and with that came a unique insight and ability
to connect. I knew then that connection formed the essence
of life. For years I couldn't think of or talk about suicide so
I undertook training in suicide-prevention skills and found

myself talking someone out of taking their own life. We spoke several times over months. Almost a year later she rang to thank me. She said: 'I don't know how you knew, but you knew.' In that moment all my past experiences made sense. I not only could, but more importantly *had* a burning desire to make a difference in the world and maybe I could combine all my skills and past experience to do that. I started working with the Black Dog Institute to help build resilience in firefighters and reduce the incidence of PTSD and suicide in emergency service workers.

'Then, even though I had no writing experience, I began to write the story of my brother and me, documented in the book *Standing on My Brother's Shoulders*. Something inherent drove me for I was living my meaning and purpose in life. That was my brother's gift to me. The face I showed to the world and my internal world became fused and I found the strength to live the life I wanted to, not the life others expected of me. For years I only saw what life took from me. Now I see what it has given me.'

Tara's story reveals many of the features of PTG – a deep sense of meaning and purpose and a desire to make a difference in the world. These are examples of eudaimonic well-being, which you can read more about in Chapter 5.

As it is normal for the positive and negative to co-exist, it may well be that while you are still going through symptoms of trauma, you may recognize some of the traits listed on page 52 beginning to take root in your own life. If so, you may already be on a PTG journey. And if not I hope these feel like worthwhile qualities to keep in mind as you make your way through the most testing of times.

Increased personal strength

There is definitely truth in the old adage that 'what doesn't kill you makes you stronger'. Dealing with a traumatic experience can consume every ounce of energy you possess and still people are able to find unknown reserves of strength within them to keep going. While facing up to the challenge of adversity can leave you feeling weak, at the same time it may actually be strengthening you in all kinds of ways – maybe initially unseen. A traumatic experience can test you to your limits but having gone through one trying situation will equip you for future difficult events. It also helps you get to know yourself better and discover what you're really capable of.

Trauma survivors often talk about having gained a deeper understanding of themselves and an increased sense of authenticity. They know who they really are and how they've changed for the better. They also refer to feeling more alive, open, empathetic and humble and that they have more compassion toward others having been through trauma themselves. This can result in a greater feeling of confidence and maturity, particularly for those who go through trauma at a young age.

Closer and more meaningful relationships

Trauma is just as much a test of our relationships as it is of ourselves. The tough times can bring you closer as you open up to loved ones and receive their support. Some relationships, however, may not survive the crisis for all kinds of reasons. For example, some people simply might not feel strong enough to face up to what you have gone through; some might not be open enough to accept a change in the dynamic of your relationship with them. It can be disappointing to discover that some people you thought would be there for you turn out not to be. But, on the other hand, you may be pleasantly surprised at unexpected kindness from others, including strangers, who rally around to support you. I remember when my mother was seriously ill I got a phone call telling me to come quickly to the hospital as the medics were concerned about her condition. It was the worst drive of my life. Three hours later I sprinted onto the ward only to find her bed was empty. A nurse, spotting my distress, scooped me up from the floor and put her arm through mine to walk me around to the other side of the ward where my mother had been moved. I'll never forget

CASESTUDY BIRTH OF A DISABLED CHILD LEADS TO MAJOR SHIFTS IN RELATIONSHIPS

When a marketing executive discovered she was expecting a child with Down's Syndrome, she was encouraged to terminate the pregnancy. She decided instead to go ahead.

'My priorities changed overnight and although it was a very stressful time, my partner and I became closer than ever. If I'd felt protective over my immediate family before, I suddenly felt a thousand times more so. My little family unit was what was important in life.

'During the last months of pregnancy, my life changed considerably. I lost a lot of "friends" – some never even contacted me after they heard the news about the baby – and I was left with only a handful of good friends. My life was stripped back but somehow it felt good – through this ordeal, through this unknown, terrifying entity, I discovered my true friends, my true self and I suddenly felt really strong.

'My family is what is important to me and I am now conscious of true friendship and feel very grateful for it.'

her kindness. Going through a traumatic experience opens you up to the importance of other people for our well-being. The superficialities of life, whether stressing to meet deadlines or preserve appearances, are swept away and you may discover a new sense of community, such as with fellow trauma survivors in support groups and internet forums. This was the experience of a local government worker in Wales after major surgery to remove a brain tumour. 'Trauma certainly helps you to sort out who your real soulmates are. And it allows you to meet amazing new people in hospital and fellow survivors as you watch each other go through rehabilitation in slow, often circular patterns. You all get used to living in "setback city" – one step forward, two back – as you learn to walk and talk and think again.'

A new appreciation for life

It's no surprise when an adversity rocks your world, such as a diagnosis of serious illness or a financial crisis, that it can prompt you to question everything, change your philosophy of life and search for new meaning. It can also greatly increase your appreciation of life itself, especially if you have been faced with the reality of your own mortality during your trauma. For some people this can act as a wake-up call, reminding them just how precious our time here on earth is and prompting them to reflect deeply on how best to make use of the time that they have remaining.

New priorities and possibilities

There is often a sense of life 'before' and 'after' a traumatic event. No surprise then that, as your life changes, so too do your priorities. You may well become less concerned with trivia which might impact on how you want to spend your time, the work you want to do and even the people you want to be around. The local government worker mentioned on

CASESTUDY LIVING WITH A LIFE-LIMITING CONDITION

An HR professional had the shock of his life when he went to the doctor to get the results of a kidney test. 'When I was told that I would only have kidney function for another 10 years, it seemed the world had collapsed on top of me. It was like an early death sentence. It was the beginning of a long battle and a fight for the life I wanted to continue to live with passion and joy. My illness has helped me understand life in all its immense beauty and fragility. Today I practise a form of gratitude every day that allows me to appreciate more and more the unexpected, wonderful surprises that life brings us as well as the immense kindness and tenderness of small gestures from others.'

page 59 lost her career but gained a new attitude. 'Before my trauma I was incredibly career-orientated, climbing ever higher. I'd think: 'Let us just get through this hour, this day, this month, this year and everything will be easier.' Now I have the opposite attitude to time; it's not something to be got through but something to be enjoyed. An hour to walk around the lake, a day for creating teaching resources, a week to explore a coastal cycle path. I don't need to hang on in there for futuristic pleasures and relaxation. I enjoy what I'm doing.'

Trauma reconnects you with what's truly important in life. You may want to spend more time on meaningful pursuits, whether that's spending time with your family, helping people in need, or ensuring you get more down time just to 'be'. This opens up a deeper kind of happiness known in psychology as 'eudaimonic well-being', which comes from living a life of meaning and purpose and which we explore in more depth on pages 132–135.

Spiritual development

A life-changing trauma, such as facing the reality of our mortality, can also result in major changes in spirituality and our philosophy in life. The crisis can prompt us to ask the big existential questions: What is the meaning of life? Is there a God? What happens when we die? What is the purpose of my life?

FOCUS ON LEARNING FROM THE DYING

The Top 5 Regrets of the Dying is a book by Bronnie Ware, an Australian palliative care nurse. Her job involved looking after patients in the last weeks of their lives. She had many special conversations during these times. 'I learnt never to underestimate someone's capacity for growth when they are faced with their own mortality. Each experienced a variety of emotions but every patient found their peace before they departed.' When she asked about regrets or things they would do differently, common themes surfaced again and again.

1 I wish I hadn't worked so hard.
2 I wish I'd stayed in touch with my friends.
3 I wish I'd let myself be happier.
4 I wish I'd had the courage to express my true self.
5 I wish I'd lived a life true to my dreams instead of what others expected of me.

These regrets reflect much of the growth experienced by the people who have shared their stories in this chapter. PTG helps people live an authentic life in touch with what is truly important to them.

Survivors often talk about experiencing spiritual growth, developing a faith in something bigger than themselves as they go through their 'long dark night of the soul'. They may decide to pray or meditate, or find comfort in the religion of their childhood or a new faith. The tsunami survivor felt a strong spiritual sensation when she came close to drowning. 'Instead of feeling any sense of panic, I felt that everything was simply fine as it was and that I would live on through my love for others and theirs for me. This has left me with a strong sense that, whatever religion we may practise, love is really all that matters and, as such, is the ultimate power.'

Some people also feel gratitude toward a divine entity for helping them get through the crisis. A sepsis survivor, who suffered the loss of both legs and several fingers, was sustained by his faith in God during seven gruelling months in hospital. 'We have been tested greatly by this episode in our life but my wife and I have found that hope and trust and our belief in God helped us through the various stages of recovery and into new seasons in our life.'

You may not necessarily experience all five of the areas of growth identified in this chapter but psychologists Tedeschi and Calhoun estimate that up to 90 per cent of trauma survivors will experience change in one of these dimensions. As mentioned by the brain tumour survivor on page 59, the journey from trauma to growth is often a case of one step forward and two back. It is highly unlikely to be the instant makeover so beloved of TV and lifestyle magazines. Trauma sends out ripples that can continue to have an impact for years. Equally, the growth may be a long time in coming but no less substantial when it finally arrives.

How does PTG happen?

PTG is thought to involve a dismantling and rebuilding of our internal world. Much of the early thinking around PTG is based on the 'Shattered Assumptions' theory (1992) developed by Prof. Ronnie Janoff-Bulman at the University of Massachusetts Amherst. The theory states that trauma destroys our benevolent view that the world is a safe, predictable and just place and that we are good and worthy people. According to the theory, trauma can cause us to reject the view that, if we do the right thing, all will turn out well in the end. Traumatic experiences, such as the death of a child or being critically injured, break these assumptions. PTG develops by engaging with this new and painful reality. Rebuilding our internal world inevitably involves a form of cognitive restructuring which includes major shifts in the way we view life and ourselves.

The process starts by trying to make sense of the trauma, which can prompt a re-evaluation of our core beliefs. In the early stages, unwelcome, automatic thoughts triggered by the traumatic experience feel intrusive. But later on this rumination shifts into something more constructive as people find some meaning in the adversity and gravitate toward a place of acceptance about their changed world, gaining wisdom and well-being along the way.

Making meaning out of the suffering is a key part of the PTG process. Highly influential in our understanding of meaning is Viktor Frankl, an Austrian psychiatrist who was imprisoned in Nazi concentration camps during World War Two and lost his wife and most of his immediate family. In his book *Man's Search for Meaning* Frankl states that 'Everything can be taken from a man but . . . the last of the human freedoms – to choose one's attitude in any given set of circumstances.' We may not always be able to control what happens to us but we can control the meaning we give to it and find some value in it. Changing how we think about what happens is at the core of modern resilience training. Finding a way to regard the adversity as a challenge to rise to will help with the process of growth.

Self-actualization – 'The actualizing tendency'
Another approach to PTG comes from British psychologists Stephen Joseph and Alex Linley, who worked at the University of Warwick in the mid-2000s. According to their 'organismic

valuing theory', people have a propensity to growth and are motivated to fulfil their potential. Adversity leads to a breakdown in the beliefs that form our identity, and PTS is the signal that we need to process the new trauma-related information on a cognitive level. PTS then becomes the catalyst for PTG, as people are naturally motivated to process the traumatic experience in ways that will maximize their psychological well-being. How you rebuild your internal world and incorporate the traumatic events into your perspective on life, will determine whether or not you experience PTG.

Assimilation v Accommodation

In his book *What Doesn't Kill Us* (2011) Stephen Joseph uses the example of a shattered vase (see box opposite) to illustrate how the process of PTG operates:

- **assimilation**, which will take you back to where you were pre-trauma, albeit in a more fragile state (like a vase re-formed from many broken fragments)
- **accommodation**, which has the potential to spur you on to positive growth and higher functioning (like a new artwork made from the fragments of the vase)

Assimilation occurs when a person maintains their pre-trauma worldview and does not alter their mental frameworks. An example of this might be a homemaker,

FOCUSON UNDERSTANDING THE 'SHATTERED VASE' METAPHOR

As mentioned opposite, Prof. Stephen Joseph uses a brilliant metaphor of mending or recycling a broken vase to explain the processes of assimilation and accommodation in response to trauma.

Imagine a lovely piece of porcelain falling and breaking into pieces. If you pick up the pieces and very carefully stick them back together, the vase may end up looking more or less like it did before, but the truth is that it will be weaker, held together with glue or sticking tape, and will be more likely to break again or to leak. This is **assimilation**. You and your life may look the same but in reality you are much more fragile.

If, on the other hand, you choose to collect all the pieces and make something new out of them such as a beautiful mosaic, the end result will be something unique and valuable in its own right. Something new has emerged from the old. This is **accommodation**. You will look and feel different but will be stronger as a result of accepting and working with the new reality.

who, after the death of her husband, feels she needs to carry on with the same role as before, or a business person who expects to be able to keep working full kilter after suffering a serious illness. This may be because they feel unable to come to terms fully with the tragedy but, unfortunately, it is likely to leave them all the more vulnerable to future stressful events as they have not been able to renegotiate their assumptions about life.

Accommodation, on the other hand, happens when someone is able to face up to and engage actively with the new reality of their post-trauma situation and rebuild their mental framework to accommodate the trauma within it. An example of this would be a widow accepting that she needs to take a new role in providing for the family after the loss of her husband, or the business person realizing that they have to alter their working patterns and/or workload after illness.

Is PTG a purely psychological process?

The gains that come with PTG extend beyond the mind to benefit the body too. Often we take our bodies for granted but the shock of a trauma such as a cancer diagnosis can reconnect us with the physical and prompt us to take better care of our bodies. Engaging with exercise, nutrition and rest not only supports healing but can help the body become stronger, more resilient and function better than it did before, as we'll see in the next chapter. Studies have shown better immune system functioning and lower cortisol levels as some of the positive physical outcomes of PTG.

We've now reached the turning point in the book where our focus shifts from learning about adversity to facilitating PTG itself. Although you may have had little or no control over the circumstances that resulted in your trauma, you do have choices over the future. What counts now is not so much what happened to you but what happens next. The chapters that follow draw on positive psychology, the science of resilience and well-being, to take you on a journey that will show you how to rise to the challenge of trauma by:

• Coping positively while in the eye of the storm
• Strengthening your resilience for times of extreme stress
• Laying down the foundations for growth

The journey from trauma to growth is not, in real life, a simple linear one. One day you might be in 'grow' mode and the next you might be back to 'cope'. I hope that the model of cope/strengthen/grow presented here proves a useful way to help you navigate through times when you're feeling lost or overwhelmed. You may well prefer to dip into the chapters at random to find tips and tools to suit how you're feeling at the time. Choose whichever way works best for you.

CHAPTER 3

How do you cope
positively during and
after trauma?

Trauma is a complex experience which means, in truth, that there is no one-size-fits-all approach to dealing with it. So, for this and the chapters that follow, I have handpicked a selection of therapies and self-help techniques which are known for being helpful in coping with trauma, managing PTS symptoms, building resilience and ultimately increasing the likelihood of PTG.

First and foremost, whether you are in the midst of trauma or in its immediate aftermath, it's important to give yourself the time and space to have what is a natural, human response to a difficult experience. Shock, grief, sadness and a sense of shattered beliefs are completely normal and in no way indicative of any weakness or failure on your part. They are, however, signals of a need for some self-care. This is more than just routine healthcare. Self-care includes any intentional actions you take to support your physical, mental and emotional health. It's about actively making deposits into your bank of resilience by nurturing your mind, body and spirit and reaching out to loved ones and people who can help you recover. All this makes coping much easier.

What might 'coping' with trauma look like?

Every trauma has its own unique features, depending on the severity of the event, its duration and the subjective experience of the survivor, but what they have in common is that they are extremely stressful experiences that stretch and overwhelm your ability to cope.

'Positive coping' involves the strategies and actions you can take to manage and reduce the stress of these challenging situations. So how do you cope positively when you are being tested to your very limits? Let me say first that there isn't a 'right' way to cope, but there are two major coping responses, which Lazarus and Folkman describe in their transactional model of stress and coping (1984). These are:

- Emotion-focused coping
- Problem-focused coping

As you read the explanations below, try to identify your own default coping style and notice whether one of the other approaches might have something to offer you.

Emotion-focused coping
This is when your attention is on the emotional distress caused by the trauma rather than on resolving the problematic situation itself. Emotion-focused coping involves trying to reduce and manage anxiety, depression, fear and other negative emotional responses. Coping strategies such as confiding in a sympathetic friend and having a good cry help us feel better even if they don't solve the issue. Not every

adversity has a solution to it, of course, nor is it within our total control – bereavement or a diagnosis of terminal illness, for example – so allowing yourself to feel and express emotions can help you adjust to the situation. Reaching out to a trusted friend or a counsellor for moral support and a shoulder to lean on are ways into emotion-focused coping. Other forms include meditation, listening to music, physical activity such as going for a walk, journalling or expressing your emotions through acts of creativity or humour. Dark humour, for example, is often used by those working in the emergency services as a way of coping with the trauma and tragedy they routinely witness. Beware, however, of the less healthy forms of emotion-focused coping such as drowning your sorrows in alcohol or over-indulging in comfort food.

Emotion-focused coping can be particularly useful in the early stages of PTS to self-soothe during high emotional distress or in circumstances that will not change and where you need to learn to accept the situation as it is.

Problem-focused coping

This coping method involves taking practical steps to move forward and resolve the issue, and can often be most helpful after an initial period of emotion-focused coping. People using problem-focused coping try to deal directly with the cause of adversity to reduce or eliminate the stress involved.

It's a more active form of coping, appropriate for situations in which you can exercise some control, such as in the case of a business failure or a toxic relationship. By shouldering the responsibility for your own well-being and developing a plan of action, you have a map to navigate your way forward. Seeking out information, evaluating the pros and cons, learning new skills and applying a solutions focus are all positive forms of taking control.

Does avoidance coping help?

PTS sufferers often engage in avoidance coping, trying to stay away from anything associated with the trauma. Although the idea of 'avoiding' your PTS may, at first, sound like a negative way to react – and it would be if you did it on a permanent basis – in the short term it can be a helpful way of disengaging from the source of distress when it's at its most overwhelming. This could take the form, for example, of going to the cinema to lose yourself in a film for a couple of hours or doing something else you like that acts as a distraction from your distress and gives you a break to regroup and marshal your inner resources. Where it becomes dysfunctional is if, over the long term, you continue to distract yourself, such as with alcohol, drugs, overwork or sex, to avoid dealing with the situation. It's a good idea to look to some of the problem-focused coping strategies to find a way to move forward.

What do you need to keep going through trauma?

The hierarchy of needs (1943) is a well-known theory in the psychology world. Abraham Maslow's quest to understand human motivation led him to formulate a list of basic needs that have to be fulfilled in order to maximize psychological health (see diagram below). The bottom layers of the pyramid represent deficiency needs, where there is a lack of something that needs to be satisfied before moving to the upper levels, which are needs for growth. I think this hierarchy feels particularly relevant to managing PTS symptoms and the journey from trauma to growth.

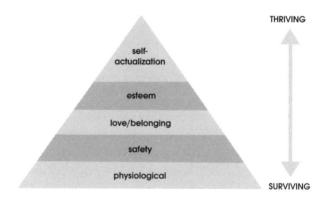

Doing what we can simply to *survive* trauma is the clear priority early on in the recovery process. This involves tending to the physiological needs at the bottom of the pyramid, such as food and sleep. Once our basic physical needs are covered, the next layer up is the need for safety – not only physical safety but a sense of psychological, social and economic safety to regain stability after trauma. Once the lower needs are met, then we can begin to move further up toward thriving.

Tending to the body is a crucial first step to recovery. Trauma lives in our bodies as well as our minds according to Bessel van der Kolk, author of *The Body Keeps the Score*. The body–mind connection is frequently underrated in the traditional Western understanding of health. Our emotions, for example, come with physical expressions – fear with a racing heart, sadness with tears, or anger with muscle tension and a clenched jaw. Traumatized people often have trouble sensing what is going on in their bodies and yet this is important for recovery. As van der Kolk puts it, 'Trauma victims cannot recover until they become familiar with and befriend the sensations in their bodies.'

Fortunately, the body can also be used as a tool to facilitate recovery from trauma and raise well-being. The rest of this chapter offers a range of ways to help you fulfil your body's needs and enhance your physical well-being before going on to address the 'higher' needs in later chapters, all of which can put you on the path to growth through adversity.

What physical steps can you take to help you feel better?

Trauma is exhausting. You may feel *emotionally* drained so self-care following trauma is especially important to keep your body strong and healthy. Admittedly, it is easier said than done to look after your body if you are in a state of anxiety, depression or hyperarousal. One thing I did when I was in the eye of the storm was to book myself weekly massages at the local college of bodywork. Physical self-care involves:

Healthy food and drink

- Eating fresh, seasonal food with at least five portions a day of fruit and vegetables.
- Keeping your water intake up to stay well hydrated. Mental exhaustion is often a sign of dehydration.
- Lowering caffeine and sugar intake as these can make you feel more anxious than you already do.

Focusing on nutrition will not only help to maintain your physical health but also positively impact your mood and therefore mental health.

Physical awareness and activity

Good mental health is built on the foundations of physical health, and regular exercise is a powerful way to improve your mood. Psychologist Tal Ben-Shahar from Harvard

University goes as far as saying that 'not exercising is like taking depressants'. According to the Green Exercise Research Team at the University of Essex, just 5–10 minutes of physical activity in a natural environment can boost your mood. I found that strolling around my local park helped me walk my way out of depression and many of my clients have also told me how a gentle physical activity, whether that be walking, swimming or yoga, has made them feel better, despite the initial mental struggle that it can sometimes take to get started.

Often with trauma we can lose the sense of our bodies as the mind gets caught up in painful memories and emotions, making us feel detached from the world. Re-tuning into the body through physical activity can help bring you back into the present and feel more grounded. Another method is simply to notice your feet making contact with the ground as you stand and walk. Mindfulness practices, such as the 'body scan' (see pages 80–81), help raise awareness of what's going on in the whole body, not just your head.

Rest and sleep

Healing from trauma is physically and mentally draining and therefore allowing yourself to rest will recharge your batteries, help you feel better and support the recovery process. If your body is in a state of continual hyperarousal it's important to

TRYIT THE BODY SCAN

The simple meditation practice below is a way of getting back in touch with your physical self. It involves 'scanning' through each part of your body to notice what's going on without seeking to change it. As well as helping you to inhabit the whole body rather than being stuck in your head, it's a good way to 'ground' yourself. There are plenty of online audio guides to the body scan, which can take around 45 minutes. Here's a three-minute version.

- Find a quiet place to sit or lie comfortably. Close your eyes and begin by bringing your attention to your body.

- Notice the weight of your body on the chair or floor.

- Take a few deep breaths. As you breathe in, let in more oxygen, to vitalize the body. Then, as you breathe out, have a sense of relaxing more deeply.

- Notice either your feet or your buttocks on the floor. Note the sensations of them touching the floor.

- Notice your legs against the chair or floor – pressure, pulsing, heaviness, lightness.

- Notice the feeling of your back against the chair or floor.

- Bring your attention into your stomach area. If your stomach is tense or tight, let it soften. Take a breath.

- Notice your hands. Are they tense or tight? See if you can allow them to soften.

- Notice your arms. Feel any sensation that is present. Let your shoulders relax.

- Notice your neck and throat. Let them be soft. Relax.

- Soften your jaw. Let your face and facial muscles relax.

- Then take notice of your whole body. Take one more breath.

- Be aware of your whole body as best you can. Take a breath. And then, when you're ready, open your eyes.

Adapted from: The Greater Good Science Center, University of California, Berkeley.

find ways to counter-balance this, as this will allow you to sleep better too. Sleep is the ultimate restorer so if yours is disturbed it's a good idea to establish a relaxing bedtime routine and try sleep hygiene practices such as:

- Switching off electronic devices at least an hour before bedtime and keep smartphones etc. out of your bedroom.
- Avoiding caffeine, alcohol and nicotine close to bedtime.
- Doing enough physical exercise during the early part of the day so that you feel naturally sleepy later on.

How can you make friends with the parasympathetic nervous system?

As explained on page 21, the sympathetic nervous system (SNS) is constantly being fired by trauma, putting us into the state of 'fight' or 'flight'. One practical way of managing the stress response is to activate the parasympathetic nervous system (PNS), which acts as the body's brake, restoring a state of relaxation and bringing the body back to normal resting levels of functioning. Making friends with the PNS will help attend to a sense of safety, the next layer up in Maslow's hierarchy of needs (see page 76).

A simple way of activating the PNS is via something we do automatically – breathing. Deep breathing is calming, the opposite to the shallow breathing that happens with acute stress. Deliberately taking time out to enjoy a few long, deep breaths – right down into the belly – can shift your state of mind, regulate emotions and reduce anxiety. Remember it is the exhalation that triggers the PNS so allow yourself to breathe out as fully as you breathe in.

Dr Emma Seppala from Stanford University has tested yoga-breathing meditations on military veterans suffering from PTSD. In a study published in the *Journal of Traumatic Stress* (2014) she found that this form of controlled breathing significantly reduced PTSD symptoms as well as anxiety. The veterans' startle responses calmed down indicating that they were suffering from fewer signs of hyperarousal. The study suggests that something as simple as a breathing technique can be a good – and less invasive – alternative or additional form of treatment for PTS.

How else can paying attention to our physical body help us cope after trauma?

Trauma is a 'psychophysical' experience according to Babette Rothschild, trauma specialist and author of *The Body Remembers*. The brain and body process, remember and perpetuate traumatic experiences even when there is no physical component involved in the adversity itself. Flashbacks, as was explained on page 37, involve the body reliving the trauma as though it were happening right now.

Although PTS has been traditionally regarded as a disorder of the mind, trauma experts such as Bessel van der Kolk and Peter Levine agree that the body is key in the understanding and healing of traumatic experiences. A new generation of trauma therapies has emerged that take this mind–body approach to healing. These include treatments such as:

- EMDR (Eye-Movement Desensitization and Reprocessing)
- EFT (Emotional Freedom Techniques) and other tapping therapies such as TFT (Thought Field Therapy)

TRYIT YOGA BREATHING TECHNIQUE

Dr Andrew Weil, a leading figure in integrative medicine, is an advocate of this simple 4–7–8 breathing practice. It's immediately relaxing, acting as an antidote to stress, and is a natural tranquillizer with benefits that accrue with practice. Sit with your back straight and place the tip of your tongue against the ridge of tissue just behind your top front teeth. Hold it there throughout the exercise. Inhale quietly through the nose and exhale audibly through the mouth.

1 First of all, exhale completely through the mouth, slightly pursing the lips to make a whoosh sound.

These therapies can bring relief in a short course of sessions without any need to dwell on the adversity itself, as is often the case with talking therapies. The memories are still there but you're no longer stuck in the moment reliving the trauma.

What is EMDR and how can it help?
EMDR was discovered quite by chance in 1987 by Dr Francine Shapiro, a psychologist from the Mental Research Institute in Palo Alto, California. She was out walking in the park while preoccupied with some painful memories

2 Close your mouth and breathe in for a count of four.

3 Hold your breath for a count of seven.

4 Exhale, making the whoosh sound, for a count of eight.

5 This is one cycle; now repeat for a further three rounds.

6 Do this practice twice a day.

Pace yourself to suit your lung capacity but always maintain the 4–7–8 ratio. With practice you can slow down and breathe more deeply. This practice also helps with sleep.

FOCUS ON WHAT HAPPENS IN AN EMDR SESSION

The treatment known as Eye-Movement Desensitization and Reprocessing (EMDR) is delivered in a course of sessions. The therapist guides the client through relaxation exercises to use in case of distress and creates an 'anchor' – a safe place to return to. The client is then asked to recall the disturbing memory and follow the therapist's finger as it passes back and forth in front of their eyes. Other forms of left–right stimulation may also be used such as taps or sounds. After each 'round' the therapist checks in with the client before continuing with the eye movements until the distress has cleared or is substantially reduced. The goal is to help the body unlock the 'frozen' traumatic memories and reprocess them. Accessing them in this way serves to 'neutralize' the memories so that the original issue is no longer disturbing and the client is able to experience more positive emotions and thoughts.

when she noticed that her eyes were moving rapidly back and forth and that this brought relief to her distress. She experimented further and found that certain eye movements reduced the intensity and anxiety of disturbing thoughts. Since then a protocol has been developed for EMDR, and it is now recommended as an effective treatment for PTSD by the World Health Organization, the American Psychiatric Association and the National Health Service in the UK.

EMDR is based on a natural function of the body – Rapid Eye Movement (REM). The mind uses REM during sleep to process the emotional experiences of the day. Traumatic memories and associated stimuli may be poorly processed and get stored in an isolated memory network as a 'memory-filing error'. REM sleep therefore fails to bring the usual relief from distress. EMDR is thought to produce an advanced stage of REM processing that can unlock the trauma. Through the eye movement the brain is able to process the emotionally charged memory and alleviate symptoms associated with it.

What is EFT and how can it help?

Since the 1980s we've witnessed the emergence of mind–body therapies collectively known as 'energy psychology', based on the concept of life force or chi/qi in traditional Chinese medicine. Among these are 'tapping therapies', which are forms of acupressure based on the same energy points as those used in acupuncture. The best known of these are Emotional Freedom Techniques (EFT), which involve gently tapping with fingertips on a sequence of meridian points on the face, hands and upper body while tuning in to a particular event or memory that holds distress or pain.

TRYIT EFT: THE BASIC RECIPE

The 'basic recipe' is an elementary EFT technique that can be used to help with all kinds of emotional issues. Gary Craig's website www.emofree.com has full instructions and a video to guide you.

- Bring to mind the source of distress and rate its intensity on a scale of 1–10.

- Design a phrase that describes the experience using this format: 'Even though I have (e.g. a fear of drowning), I deeply and completely accept myself.'

- Say the phrase three times while tapping using two or three fingers on the fleshy point on the side of the hand (the 'karate chop' point).

- Choose a short version of this sentence as the 'reminder phrase' (e.g. 'fear of drowning').

- Next tap each of the following acupressure points 5–7 times while saying the reminder phrase out loud:

- Top of the head

- Beginning of the eyebrow (inner edge)

- Side of the eye

- Under the eye

- Under the nose

- Chin point

- Beginning of the collarbone (inner edge)

- Under the arm (on a line with the nipple)

- Test the intensity of the issue by rating it again from 1–10 to get a sense of progress. Continue with more rounds until the intensity goes down to zero or plateaus at a low level.

The evidence for EFT's efficacy as a treatment for PTS looks promising. There have been several randomized control trials conducted with military veterans which show substantial improvements in their symptoms of PTSD, anxiety and depression, and a reduction in their levels of cortisol, the stress hormone.

Sometimes referred to as 'psychological acupressure', EFT reduces the intensity of emotional trauma, lowering stress levels and the symptoms of hyperarousal. An American named Gary Craig devised EFT in the 1990s, inspired by Thought Field Therapy (TFT), a tapping technique developed by psychologist Dr Roger Callahan. EFT is based on the notion that the cause of negative emotions is a disruption in the body's energy system and that tapping on meridians will help to release blockages and clear unresolved issues. The advantages of using tapping are that it is simple, non-invasive and rapid-acting. EFT is effective within a few sessions without the need to revisit the traumatic experience over and over again, flooding the body with stress hormones each time. In a similar way to EMDR, you will still remember the trauma but it is no longer as charged as it was before. EFT can be self-administered but it is advisable to work with a qualified therapist first of all so that you can experience EFT within a safe space before using it as a self-help tool.

In summary

The major theme in this chapter has been that the body can be used as an *instrument* for healing trauma. The positive news is that the benefits don't stop there. Dr Kate Hefferon from the University of East London has identified, through her work with cancer survivors, three main ways in which people can also experience PTG *related* to the body – there can be some kind of physical improvement post-trauma. Known as 'corporeal post-traumatic growth', this can show up as:

- **A new, improved relationship with the body.** Having a serious illness can act as a 'wake-up call' to stop taking our bodies for granted and treat them with kindness. As we become more aware of the body, we are more likely to handle it with increased care. Taking exercise, for example, can result in regaining and even surpassing previous levels of physical functioning.
- **Greater awareness of health-related behaviour.** Trauma survivors have a stronger sense of the importance of the body and are therefore more likely to engage in healthy practices such as eating well and give up damaging habits like smoking and excessive alcohol consumption.
- **Stronger in mind as well as body.** After experiencing trauma many people report that making positive changes to their *physical health* also led to them functioning better *psychologically*, such as feeling more mentally alert and having greater optimism toward the future.

Now that we've explored a range of ways to help us cope in the eye of the storm, in the next chapter we'll look at how we can work on strengthening our resilience so that we feel better equipped to face up to what life throws at us.

CHAPTER 4

How can you strengthen your resilience to keep going through adversity?

Bad things happen. But while some people go under when faced with adversity, others find a way through and are able to bounce back from the crisis. The key difference between these groups is what is known as *resilience* – having the inner strength to keep going while the winds of adversity threaten to topple you. In this chapter we turn our attention from body-based practices to some of the more mind-focused therapies that can fortify us to move through adversity and sow the seeds of growth.

What exactly do we mean by resilience?

Resilience is about maintaining and regaining psychological well-being in the face of adversity, trauma, tragedy and other major sources of stress such as serious health problems or overwhelming work pressures. There is a wide variety of definitions of resilience but psychologists agree on there being three main types:

- **Resistance resilience.** The ability to stand strong while going through adversity, like having your feet planted firmly on the ground.

- **Recovery resilience**, also known as 'bouncebackability'. Being able to rebound to the level of functioning you had prior to the adversity, like the tree that bends and sways in a storm.

- **Reconfiguration resilience.** The changes that occur through adversity which can improve someone's capacity to cope with subsequent challenges. This can be a stepping stone to PTG.

The good news is that resilience is not something you're either born with or not – it's something you can learn. Dr Karen Reivich, co-author of *The Resilience Factor*, describes resilience as 'a group of positive characteristics, abilities and resources' and teaches seven skills – emotion regulation, impulse control, optimism, flexible thinking, self-efficacy (confidence in problem-solving), empathy and reaching out (to take appropriate risks). Neither is resilience some rare quality. Prof. Ann Masten, from the University of Minnesota, refers to it as 'ordinary magic' because resilience arises from a range of common factors such as close relationships or a brain that's functioning OK.

Resilience is much more common than you might imagine. Prof. George Bonanno from Columbia University has carried out research into traumatic experiences such as the death of a spouse and the events of 9/11. His research suggests that the most widespread reaction to trauma or loss is not PTSD as you might first think, but is, in fact, resilience. Even with troops heading into a war zone, the most 'common' consequence of high adversity is a brief episode of depression and anxiety before a return to previous levels of functioning. This particular insight comes from Prof. Martin Seligman, who works with the United States Army on the Comprehensive Soldier Family Fitness (CSFF) programme, which aims to build resilience in service personnel and their families.

The relationship, however, between resilience and PTG is not clear-cut. Some studies suggest that the higher your resilience, the less likely you are to experience PTG as you have less of the struggle with trauma, the mechanism that triggers PTG. I prefer to take the pragmatic view that the actions that build resilience will also strengthen your chances of the positive transformation that is PTG.

Can we take steps to build resilience?

The first thing to note is that you already have a resilience resource available to you and that is YOU. The way you coped in the past will help you cope in the future. As a starter try this: Take a few minutes to think back over your life decade by decade. Then get a pen and a large piece of paper, and draw a lifeline, plotting the major events and turning points on it. Now ask yourself what you did that helped you get through the difficult times. What can you learn from the past that might serve you in the future? The SSRI exercise on pages 98–99 draws on the precious resource that is your previous experience.

Who is your Resilience Hero?

Think about someone in your life who could serve as a role model of resilience for you. Maybe a member of your family – an aunt, uncle or grandparent? Someone you know through work? Or even someone in public life? What strengths did they draw upon to help them through their time of crisis?

For me it would be my grandmother, an agricultural worker in northern France with 12 children and a farm to look after. During World War Two, while being evacuated from the farm, she survived a piece of shrapnel lodging in her neck after an air raid. She was a Resilience Hero for me because of her stoical, down-to-earth nature and her great spirit – she was able to find lightness even in the gloomiest times.

Another personal Resilience Hero for me would be Nelson Mandela, who was incarcerated for 27 years but somehow kept the faith and went on to become President of South Africa on his release. His strengths must surely include perseverance, justice and leadership, demonstrated in his own PTG journey from surviving prison to thriving as the nation's leader.

Whose tale of endurance inspires *you*? And what lessons can you learn from how they managed and bounced back from their time of adversity?

TRYIT SSRIs: YOUR PERSONAL RESILIENCE TOOLKIT

The term SSRIs normally refers to a group of antidepressants, the Selective Serotonin Reuptake Inhibitors: Prozac is one. Here they stand for **Strategies, Strengths, Resources and Insights** – all elements that can strengthen our resilience.

Think back to a difficult situation in the past that you got through in a way you now feel satisfied with. What helped you do this? What were the:

- **Strategies** you used? Practical things like asking for help, problem-solving approaches, self-care.

Can mindfulness help build resilience?

Trauma can hold us in a pattern of reliving distress over and over. When we have persistent upsetting experiences, we can end up reacting more emotionally to situations that others might not find disturbing. This can feel very intense and make it more difficult to manage our emotions and behaviour. The key difference between a traumatized brain and a resilient one is this 'emotional reactivity'. Mindfulness is an ancient form of mind-training that can help address this difficult issue.

- **Strengths** you drew upon? Your inner resources such as courage and perseverance.

- **Resources** you turned to? The external sources you relied on for guidance, inspiration or support. This could be friends, family, colleagues, mentors, professionals, support groups, helplines, internet forums and organizations.

- **Insights** you found useful? Positive ideas, perspectives and philosophies that helped you through. It could even be a phrase such as 'This too will pass,' or the PTG classic, 'What doesn't kill you makes you stronger.'

Adapted from *Find Your Power*, Chris Johnstone, 2010

Originally a spiritual practice in Buddhism, mindfulness meditation has evolved into a secular practice for health, largely through the clinical work of Dr Jon Kabat-Zinn. Mindfulness means being present and Kabat-Zinn's interpretation is based on awareness as 'paying attention in a particular way, in the present moment, on purpose, non-judgementally'. In the 1970s Kabat-Zinn began testing mindfulness techniques for the management of chronic pain and other difficult-to-treat conditions at the University of Massachusetts Medical Center. He then went on to develop an eight-week programme of mindfulness, body awareness and yoga, known as Mindfulness-Based Stress Reduction (MBSR).

Mindfulness focuses attention on awareness of the inside and its relationship to the outside – noticing the thoughts, sights, sounds, smells, tastes and touch that we experience; and accepting all such experience non-judgmentally even if it is painful. With practice, this can enhance our ability to notice what's going on without being sucked into the drama of it, so we become more of an observer of our thoughts and feelings. This type of awareness can help to strengthen resilience in two main ways:

- With **reactivity.** Mindfulness can help interrupt the vicious cycle of looping thoughts, feelings and behaviours reinforcing each other. With practice it helps you become more of an observer, creating a gap between what happens and how you react so that there is greater potential for a more balanced response. This helps to dampen down emotional reactivity.

- With **rumination**. Traumatic experiences can keep you trapped in the past, brooding over what happened, or anxiously over-thinking the future. When you are stuck in a thinking track that pulls you down, winds you up or stresses you out, mindfulness can help you gain some distance from the domination of trauma-related intrusive thoughts and feelings and instead remain calm and more in the moment.

Mindfulness approaches now form part of a variety of mental health programmes and these can be useful for trauma survivors to address PTS symptoms and associated issues such as depression and anxiety. The following courses are worth investigating:

MBSR (mindfulness-based stress reduction) has been shown to help people manage the stress that is associated with physical health conditions and is now a recognized treatment for anxiety and depression, frequently present in PTSD sufferers.

MBCT (mindfulness-based cognitive therapy) draws upon both mindfulness and cognitive therapy techniques (for these, see pages 104–105) and aims to reduce the risk of relapsing into depression.

ACT (acceptance and commitment therapy) helps people develop psychological flexibility to accept what has happened and facilitate behaviour change (see the Try It box on page 119).

TRYIT A BASIC MINDFULNESS EXERCISE

This exercise is a simple introduction to mindfulness:

- Find a comfortable position either lying down or sitting cross-legged with a straight back and shoulders relaxed.

- Ask yourself: 'What is going on with me at the moment?'

- Allow yourself to be with whatever arises for you. Acknowledge what you notice with gentleness and kindness. For example, 'This is a moment of sadness,' or 'I'm noticing anger in this moment.' And in the spirit of self-compassion, remind yourself that this is part of life, 'It's OK to feel like this, it's part of the human experience.'

- Sounds and bodily sensations may also call for your attention and, as best as you can, simply notice these experiences with openness and curiosity as they come and go, flux and change.

A note of caution – mindfulness involves leaning into experience, and this raised awareness does carry a risk of triggering initial distress or the emergence of unprocessed trauma. Having said that, mindfulness can also help people

- If particular thoughts or sensations keep pushing for your attention, see if it's possible to allow that to be OK, without judging yourself or giving yourself a hard time.

- Then, when you're ready, invite your attention to notice the sensations of the body and the pattern of your breathing. Just follow the rhythmic movement and return to the breath whenever the mind wanders, which it will do.

- If strong emotions or memories of painful events occur, see if it's possible to acknowledge these as well as any related sensations in the body and say something like, 'I can notice this is fear, and feel it in my chest. My heart is beating faster' etc. Then gently allow your awareness to drop back to your breathing, placing one hand on your belly, if this feels comfortable, and watching each new breath in and old breath out. Continue to use the breath as a place to return to when the mind gets caught up with thinking or worrying, so that these memories and feelings gradually decrease in intensity and frequency.

increase their distress tolerance so that they are more able to 'stay with' memories and symptoms that come up. It's advisable to join a mindfulness course run by a qualified instructor who can guide you through any difficulties.

Which psychological therapy is most recommended for resilience and recovery?

Cognitive-behavioural therapy (CBT) is at the core of many resilience programmes and is the most widely prescribed psychological therapy for PTSD. This talking therapy is based on the interaction between thoughts, emotions and behaviours. How the way you think (cognition) affects how you feel (emotion) and how you act (behaviour) and vice versa in each case. This can escalate so, for example, someone who *feels* nervous about a meeting may *think* that they might not be able to make their points clearly and that might make them *feel* more anxious, which in turn might make them *think* that it will be a disaster, which might make them *behave* by not going at all. CBT can help you understand how certain thoughts about your trauma can trigger PTS symptoms. By challenging and replacing negative automatic thoughts that trauma survivors have, such as 'Nowhere is safe', 'I'm going mad' or 'I'm dead inside', CBT may help them learn to cope with feelings of anger, fear and guilt.

The aim of CBT is to identify the blind spots in our thinking patterns that can trigger a big emotional reaction, by falling into thinking traps such as these:

All-or-nothing thinking: Viewing things in extreme or in black and white, such as thinking 'This mistake will ruin everything.'

Catastrophizing: Predicting the worst outcome possible. 'My heart is beating so fast it must mean I'm going to die.'

Emotional reasoning: Mistaking feelings for facts and believing that what you feel must be true, so if you feel like a failure it is because you are.

Jumping to conclusions: Making a negative interpretation of a situation even though there are no definite facts to support your assumption.

Mental filtering: Picking out a single negative detail, dwelling on it and therefore viewing the whole situation as negative.

Personalizing: Seeing yourself as the cause of some negative external event when you had little or no responsibility.

How can positive psychology build resilience?

Positive psychology is a practical science that not only builds well-being but is also known as the science of resilience. Many of its evidence-based practices can feed your reservoir of resilience. Three areas are especially helpful:

- recognizing and applying your strengths
- cultivating and enjoying more positive emotions
- practising optimism

FOCUS ON UNDERSTANDING THE ABC OF RESILIENCE

An important CBT-based skill taught on many resilience courses is what is known as the ABC. This helps people understand the relationship between what happens and its impact on our thoughts, feelings and behaviour.

A: Activating event – an adversity or event that tests your resilience. These are the facts of the situation.

B: The heat-of-the-moment **Belief** about what happened.

C: The **Consequences** for emotions (how you felt) and behaviour (what you did).

We tend to think that when adversity strikes, it has direct consequences on how we feel and behave, that we

Recognizing your strengths

We all have strengths as well as weaknesses but a crisis often means that we lose sight of the positive side of our nature. Strengths like courage, perseverance and hope can come into their own when you are navigating tough times. These qualities can be deployed to build resilience. Clinical psychologist Dr Tayyab Rashid, from the University go straight from A (the 'Activating Event') to C (the 'Consequences'). However, there is a middle stage: this is B, the 'Belief' associated with the activating event. It is this, not the adversity itself, that drives the consequences. Consider a relationship break-up, involving two people. If person 1's belief is 'I'll never find love again' the consequences might be that they feel devastated (emotion) and withdraw from the world (behaviour). Whereas if person 2's belief is 'I'm free at last' the consequences might be somewhat different. They may feel relieved (emotion) and join a dating website (behaviour). The same adversity is at work but with different beliefs driving different consequences. We can't always do something about the adversity but we can change our beliefs about it. If we are willing to challenge how we think about the adversity this will lead to different consequences for our emotions and behaviour. An important part of resilience is therefore being flexible in our thinking.

of Toronto, suggests that you can marshal your strengths to undo troubles. A strength in kindness or social intelligence, for example, might help mend a strained relationship.

Doctors are sometimes guilty of labelling patients according to their symptoms, referring to someone as a 'depressive' for instance, but if you search for someone's strengths in addition to their symptoms, you understand more of the whole person. The strengths approach to resilience is in two parts: firstly getting to know these positive qualities in yourself, then using your strengths in life (see also the box opposite).

Cultivating positive emotions

Emotions are not just something we feel, they also serve a purpose. Negative emotions act as our survival mechanism in that they alert us to danger. Anger prompts us to defend ourselves ('fight') while fear makes us look for an escape ('flight'; see page 21). When you're going through a traumatic experience the very idea of having a positive emotion may seem remote, but highly resilient people are, surprisingly, able to experience positive emotions alongside negative emotions, even in difficult situations.

Prof. Barbara Fredrickson of the University of North Carolina describes the function of joy, excitement, amusement etc. as the 'inner reset button' because they counteract the cardiovascular effects of negativity such as raised blood pressure. So watching a comedy or playing a fun game with a friend can provide relief on a bad day.

Our brains are, however, wired to notice what's wrong before we notice what's right, a part of the safety mechanism that kicks in whenever we're under threat. So we're aware of the

TRYIT DISCOVER YOUR CHARACTER STRENGTHS

There are 24 universal strengths of character, according to Chris Peterson and Martin Seligman, who led a mammoth project to chart all of humanity's positive qualities. We have all of these strengths present in us and they are open for development.

Each strength is located in one of six 'virtues'. By recognizing and focusing on developing your strengths you can access these virtues. You can take the free test and find out more at www.viasurvey.org.

WISDOM	COURAGE	TRANSCENDENCE
Creativity	Bravery	Appreciation of
Curiosity	Perseverance	beauty and
Judgment	Honesty	excellence
Love of learning	Zest	Gratitude
Perspective		Hope
		Humour
		Spirituality
JUSTICE	TEMPERANCE	HUMANITY
Teamwork	Forgiveness	Love
Fairness	Humility	Kindness
Leadership	Prudence	Social
	Self-regulation	intelligence

runaway car heading our way and are not distracted by appreciating the beautiful view. As a result, when something difficult happens the combination of the nature of emotion and the 'negativity bias' means that you can easily end up mired in negative emotions such as sadness and frustration. This means that we need to apply a bit of effort to cultivate positive emotions and overcome the brain's negativity bias.

FOCUSON PRACTICES FOR POSITIVE EMOTIONS

There is widespread scientific recognition that the following practices can increase your experience of positive emotions.

Gratitude – ask yourself these three questions daily. What is good in my life? What am I grateful for? What has gone well? Or keep a gratitude journal. Gratitude is about actively tuning in and taking notice of what is positive.

Savouring – maximize your enjoyment by slowing down and using your senses to engage fully with every positive experience. Bask, relish, marvel, luxuriate, treasure and so on.

Meditation – mindfulness and loving-kindness meditations are particularly good ways to cultivate positive emotions

Mindfulness meditation is one way to do this. Eight weeks of MBSR (see pages 100–101) has been shown to increase activity in the left prefrontal cortex, an area of the brain associated with positive emotions, and reduce the activity of the right prefrontal cortex, which is related to negative emotions. I experienced this myself through MBSR. I felt as though my brain had been subtly rewired for happiness.

and don't require mental acrobatics. See pages 102–103 for more information.

Positive relationships – cherish your loved ones and make them your priority; you need many more positive than negative emotional events in a relationship for it to flourish.

Altruism – volunteer your time to help someone out. Acts of kindness make both the giver and recipient feel good.

Time in nature – spending regular time in the great outdoors produces positive emotions in a matter of minutes.

Physical activities – exercise of any kind can provide you with an instant mood lift. Make sure it's something that brings you pleasure rather than pain.

Practising optimism

It is entirely understandable that a traumatic experience might shatter any underlying sense of optimism you have about life; it may feel hard to think positively about the future for a while. But the trouble with pessimistic thinking is that, over time, it carries a high risk of leading to depression.

Practising optimistic thinking will feed your resilience and help you orient toward PTG over the long term. And it is possible to raise your optimism level, as Martin Seligman explains in his classic book *Learned Optimism.* The neuroplasticity of the brain demonstrates that what 'fires together wires together'. This means that when brain cells communicate frequently, the connection between them strengthens. And with enough repetition these connections become automatic, whether in a positive or negative way.

The more we ruminate on a negative thought, the more entrenched that negativity becomes. This is why it can be so hard to stop depressive thoughts until we find a way of interrupting the process. We can, however, harness this pattern and learn how to think more optimistically. Although this may be a struggle at first, the more you do it the easier it will become. I think of myself as a practising optimist rather than a natural-born one and it has made a significant difference in my life.

The version of optimism that Seligman describes in *Learned Optimism* is called 'explanatory' or 'attributional style'. This is based on the way we think about the causes of events that happen to us and how we explain them to ourselves.

A **pessimist** is likely to think of the causes of a negative event as being:

- *personal* ('It's all my fault.')
- *permanent* ('It's never going to change.')
- *pervasive* ('It's ruined everything.')

An **optimist**, on the other hand, will think of the same negative event in the opposite way. The cause is

- *not personal* ('There were other factors that played a role.')
- *not permanent* ('This too will pass.')
- *not pervasive* ('Other areas of my life are going well.')

Try to challenge any patterns of pessimistic thinking that you notice in yourself and think more like an optimist using these three dimensions. After a while, it should feel more natural.

What are the three Ds of Resilience?

Earlier in this chapter we explored the ABC of resilience. Now I'd like to add another letter into this process:

The D of resilience is for

- *Disputation*
- *Distraction*
- *Distancing*

Disputation

Seligman recommends getting to know your habitual thinking patterns and challenging the negative explanations of negative events. We do this by 'disputing' the B – the 'heat of the moment' belief sparked by any negative event. There are three ways of doing this.

Examining the evidence: What's the evidence for and/or against this belief? This is accurate thinking.

Considering the alternatives: Are there other, more optimistic explanations for what has happened? This helps develop flexible thinking.

Putting things into perspective: Is there a way of ensuring that things haven't been blown out of proportion in your mind? What action can you take to move things forward?

This process of challenging pessimistic explanations will really help to develop your optimistic 'muscle'.

Distraction

Distraction techniques can involve anything from picking up the phone to talk to a friend, to making a cup of tea, to going for a walk. Doing something different like this allows you to calm down and regroup.

Distancing

'Distancing' might mean physically removing yourself from something that is upsetting by, for example, simply stepping out of the room, or applying the distance of time and coming back to the situation at a point in the future when things feel a little less charged. This approach helps prevent you from being set back by strong negative emotions when you're in the grip of a bad experience.

In summary

In this chapter we have looked at a range of strategies that I hope will help you maintain and raise the level of your resilience to help you move through times of adversity. In the final chapter, we will bring all the knowledge together to take things to the next stage; exploring ways to facilitate post-traumatic growth itself.

CHAPTER 5

How can you grow
from adversity?

'New beginnings are often disguised as painful endings.' So said Lao Tzu, the ancient Chinese philosopher and founder of Taoism, offering a beacon of hope for anyone going through a period of adversity. The new field of post-traumatic growth shows that this is just as true in the 21st century as it was over 2,000 years ago.

While the chapters up until now have focused on coping and building resilience, the following pages are about life *after* trauma and starting to nurture the post-traumatic growth that can transform your world.

What does the journey from adversity to growth involve?

The path from adversity to growth is often not a linear one; at times something might suddenly set you back to feeling barely able to cope. Such setbacks are par for the course so try not to be discouraged when they happen and instead remember that they are a normal part of striving to overcome what life has put in your way. Trauma, grief and loss have their own rhythm and 'being positive' can feel like a tyranny. The green shoots of growth may already be present amid the suffering so try to let go of any 'shoulds' and treat yourself kindly.

The five stages of loss, according to the model put forward by psychiatrist Elisabeth Kübler-Ross in her 1969 book *On Death*

TRYIT ACCEPTANCE AND COMMITMENT THERAPY (ACT)

ACT is a therapy that uses mindfulness techniques to help people open up to, rather than avoid, any unpleasant or traumatic experiences and choose a course of action that takes them forward. In a nutshell, ACT is about:

Accepting your reactions – allowing thoughts to come and go without struggling with them.

Choosing a direction – what would you like to happen?

Taking action – setting goals and committing to them.

You can't change what happened but you can change what happens next.

and Dying, are denial, anger, bargaining, depression and acceptance. It doesn't necessarily happen in that order and the model itself has been challenged over the years, but these stages also capture something of the journey to post-traumatic growth. It's the last one (acceptance) that is key to moving on from trauma.

This was the case for the sepsis survivor we met in Chapter 2. 'My journey to recovery started with acceptance. Being told that both my legs would be amputated and that I would lose most of my fingertips was shocking news. I needed to find peace amidst this entire horrid situation. It wasn't easy and even though my illness was not my fault, accepting the situation helped me to move forward.' Accepting that life is different now is the step that opens up the gateway to what happens next.

How can you start taking active steps toward growth?

Prof. Stephen Joseph, author of *What Doesn't Kill Us*, summarizes the evidence for what people need to do to move forward from adversity as:

- Confront reality (rather than deny it)
- Accept that misfortune has happened
- Take responsibility in the aftermath for how you live your life

Below are some practices that can help facilitate the next step of turning trauma into growth:

- Constructive rumination
- Telling your story
- Adopting a 'growth mindset'

Constructive rumination

As we now know, traumatic events can shatter an individual's beliefs about the world, leading people to question their lives. Early on this 'rumination' may take the form of brooding about the causes of the distress, asking 'Why me?' or trying to figure out the crucial elements that sparked the crisis. The mind understandably gets caught up in a conflict between the old sense of self pre-trauma and the new reality post-trauma. Over time, however, the rumination can shift to become more deliberate and constructive, taking stock of life, examining the self and searching for meaning.

You can get to a sense of meaning by asking yourself if there is anything at all to take away, so to speak, from the traumatic event – the silver lining in the adversity. It may take a period of reflection before an answer eventually emerges but the bonus is that it may also lead to a new sense of purpose. I know for myself that I have made meaning from episodes of depression by putting the lessons learnt into my work as a positive psychologist. My purpose in life now is to put people on the path to happiness. Do you have a sense of purpose?

Making meaning from trauma is part of 'benefit-finding', the perception of major positive changes occurring as a result of challenging life events. As we explored in earlier chapters, these benefits include a new appreciation of your own strength and resilience, being clearer about what's really important in life, becoming more compassionate or altruistic, feeling emotionally closer to family and friends, a new openness to spiritual experience, redirected priorities or simply learning to appreciate the little things more. The outcome of benefit-finding can be significant shifts in the way we relate to the world, with reconstructed mental maps of our *inner* world altering how we are toward the *outer* world. And with an extra benefit – a sprinkling of wisdom.

Telling your story

Humans are sense-making creatures. We construct stories in the search for meaning, and to generate a new narrative when trauma takes away the picture of how we expected life to be. Trying to put the adversity into words, either to a trusted person such as a therapist or friend or by journalling about it, can be a powerful step to healing from trauma. A number of our case studies came to writing as a result of a traumatic experience (see pages 54–55 for one example).

You may already be aware of the benefits of journalling as a healing therapy – in the bestselling book *The Artist's Way* Julia Cameron recommends doing 'Morning Pages' – writing about whatever crosses your mind as a stream of consciousness. And writing a 'gratitude journal' can help you tune into and savour the positives in life.

TRY IT EXPRESSIVE WRITING

Expressive writing is a form of therapy developed by Prof. James Pennebaker at the University of Texas at Austin. People are invited to write about their trauma, what it meant to them and the feelings it generated, in 15–20 minute sessions over four consecutive days. Although people may feel upset during the process, later on they often experience an improvement in psychological well-being and physical health.

Want to give it a go? Set aside 20 minutes in a quiet place to write about any important emotional issue that is affecting you. Write by hand or on the computer and have soft music in the background if you want. As you write really let go and explore your deepest emotions and thoughts. You might mention your relationships with others; your past, present or future; who you have been or who you are now. It's up to you whether you write about the same issues each day or about different topics. Don't worry about grammar or sentence structure. The only rule is that once you begin writing, you continue until the time is up.

Based on *Pennebaker's Expressive Writing Paradigm*

Adopt a 'growth mindset'

The humanistic psychologists in the mid-20th century did much to develop the notion of 'growth'. As mentioned on pages 65–66, we humans can benefit from the 'actualizing tendency', the natural driving force within us to 'expand, develop, mature', to fulfil our potential if the right conditions are present. These include an environment that supports

---

CASESTUDY **STEPS TO A NEW STORY**

A BBC reporter on a rural cycle ride nearly died after he collided with a delivery van head-on. He was severely injured and had to spend three weeks in intensive care. Two years later he is now fully recovered but feels he has undergone significant change.

'I view life differently now. As a journalist I see news stories in a changed way, what's important and what's not have shifted. I see the human story behind a tragedy much more than I ever did. I have a greater understanding. On a wider scale I think I'm more relaxed and slightly more tolerant in life. I appreciate things for what they are and I'm more able to live in the moment. My personal views have changed too and I know small things don't matter.

genuineness (openness and self-disclosure), acceptance (being viewed with unconditional positive regard) and empathy (being listened to and understood).

Prof. Carol Dweck, a leading researcher on motivation at Stanford University, has brought a new understanding to the concept of growth. Her work has shown that there are

'I have thought often about what life means and what it is, how precious it is and how close I came to not having it. I want to try and do as much as I can, enjoy as much as I can, because this has taught me that it won't be for ever; life could end at any moment. As I recovered I was keen to look up friends who I'd begun to lose touch with. I met with several of them and that was very satisfying.

'People with head injuries often change their lives totally, and can live to regret it later. I was told about this early on and experienced it myself. I wanted to go and work for a charity, or do something I thought was worthwhile, give something back to the community. I still have a desire to do something more meaningful with my life but realize that my current job isn't without meaning or purpose. When the opportunity comes up, I'll be ready to jump.'

two types of mindset that shape our lives and these are based on the beliefs that we have about our abilities:

- The fixed mindset
- The growth mindset

Although this theory was originally geared toward understanding the ingredients of success, it also has a lot to offer when it comes to thinking about how we respond to setbacks. People with a 'fixed mindset' believe that their abilities are set in stone and not open to much development in the course of their lives. So we're all born a certain unchangeable way – smart, sporty, creative, etc. Their response to setbacks tends to be to behave in a corresponding fixed way, doing the same things over and over, feeling increasingly hopeless and helpless until they eventually give up.

Someone with a 'growth mindset', on the other hand, believes that their abilities are like plants and that with enough effort, motivation and application, they can learn, develop and grow. When they have a setback they tend to behave in a more flexible way, trying different strategies to navigate toward the goal. They don't take failure as personally as someone in a fixed mindset; they learn from things going wrong and have more self-compassion.

People in a growth mindset know the value of effort and are more likely to experiment, whereas someone with a fixed mindset is likely to be too anxious about not getting it right to allow themselves the space to try something out of their comfort zone.

The good news is that simply *knowing* about the existence of a growth mindset helps to develop one. When you're starting to rebuild your life like the phoenix rising from the ashes, making the conscious decision to adopt a growth mindset can be invaluable.

Some useful ways of doing this include:

- Being open to trying new things, for example signing up for a new course, or saying yes rather than no to unexpected invitations
- Reminding yourself of the growth mindset when you meet new challenges in life
- Aiming for progress rather than perfection
- Recognizing the power of the word 'yet', as in the affirmation 'I've not succeeded *yet*'
- Praising yourself for the effort you put in to build the motivation and resilience to continue

How can I develop the five key areas of PTG?

Remember the five dimensions that psychologists Tedeschi and Calhoun identified as being part of PTG on page 52?

- Personal strength
- Closer relationships
- Greater appreciation of life
- New possibilities
- Spiritual development

The good news is that changes in these areas are likely to happen naturally over time, but there are also some simple actions you can take to nurture them actively. Some of these have already been mentioned, but I hope you'll find it useful to consider them in direct relation to the model of transformative growth first outlined in Chapter 2.

Developing personal strength

Your greatest potential for growth comes from developing your strengths rather than focusing on fixing your weaknesses. For anyone rebuilding their life after trauma it's helpful to look to your strengths for a clue as to how to move forward in the most positive direction. They represent you at your best – your positive characteristics (personal or character strengths) and your talents (performance strengths). Finding new ways to use these character strengths has been found to increase well-

TRYIT APPLYING YOUR STRENGTHS

Recognizing and using your strengths makes it more likely that you will excel with ease because you're drawing on something that comes naturally to you.

You can apply your strengths like levers to reach goals:

How might your strength in _____ help you achieve the goal of _____?

And you can also apply them to help you resolve issues:

How might your strength in _____ help you solve the problem of _____?

being and lower depression symptoms. See the box above and also page 109 for a link to a free character strengths test.

Nurturing closer relationships

Reaching out to others is an important thing to do during recovery from trauma; having a shoulder to lean on and someone to support you pays dividends when you are at your most vulnerable.

Research shows that the happiest people have good, close relationships and active social lives, which demonstrates the importance of meaningful human connection for our well-being. One very simple way to nurture relationships is to prioritize time with the people you value. For love to flourish requires a ratio of 5 to 1 positive to negative interactions according to relationship researcher John Gottman. Here are some simple ways to cultivate positive interactions with others:

- Cherish the people in your life – focus on their positives.
- Appreciate what other people do for you.
- Show empathy and compassion when others are suffering.
- Be kind to others in your everyday interactions.
- Avoid behaviours that wreck relationships, such as criticism, defensiveness, contempt and stonewalling.

Enjoying greater appreciation of life

Having your life or well-being feel threatened in some way can certainly stop you from taking it for granted. As such, gratitude is a frequent outcome of PTG. Pro-active gratitude practices include counting your blessings – such as listing three good things a day (see page 110) or writing a gratitude journal – a diary of all the positive events in your life, which you can savour whenever you need a boost. I've been keeping gratitude journals for over 20 years and it has changed my life. I went from having a scarcity mindset,

aware of everything that was *missing* in my life, to a much
happier abundance mindset, appreciating what I *do* have.

Searching out and embracing new possibilities
As one door closes another one does open . . . eventually.
It just requires patience and the willingness to act on the

CASESTUDY A NEW PURPOSE IN LIFE

The mother we met on page 58 has found that,
despite the hardship of having a disabled child, life
has changed for the better. 'I look on this ordeal as an
awakening – I honestly feel a newfound strength, as if
I could deal with ANYTHING that life throws at me. I don't
let silly, insignificant things get to me any more and if I
find myself ruminating on what people have or haven't
said or done, I now check myself and shrug it off.

'Going through this hardship cemented my intent to
do some good, to give back to the world somehow.
It inspired me to learn how to teach resilience to other
carers of children with disabilities. This desire to help
others – through my experience with my son – has
given me a new purpose in life.'

opportunities as they arise. Being flexible and accepting that things change will help you with starting a new chapter post-trauma. How can you make the most of what there is now? How can you develop a fresh plan for each of the main areas of life such as work, home, relationships, leisure and so on? Perhaps try to identify a new set of short-, medium- and long-term goals to strive for a sense of progress.

Deepening spiritual development

Trauma can often lead people to struggle with their faith, as their beliefs are shattered and they feel let down. But when they've made peace with the trauma they may experience a deepening of faith and find themselves drawn to a *more spiritual* life. You can foster this new faith by making space for regular spiritual practice, e.g. prayer, meditation or some other form of worship. Explore the world's religions by reading their sacred texts, going on retreats or connecting with a faith community. If you prefer a more secular version of spirituality you might join a philosophy group or spend time in nature.

How do you know when you're starting to grow from adversity?

Having come through a period of crisis, at some point you may begin to recognize positive changes in yourself – such as feeling stronger or more resilient. Or you may be surprised to find an unexpected 'gift' emerging, such as a newfound sense of authenticity: you know what you really want from life now; you know who your true friends are and those you can afford to let go of.

I'd like to end this book by sharing what I consider to be one of the greatest gifts of PTG, an undervalued form of happiness that often emerges, known as 'eudaimonic well-being'. This is a concept that originated with the ancient Greek philosopher Aristotle and was about living a life of virtue, but the modern definition is something closer to flourishing and fulfilment. 'Eudaimonia' is an umbrella term describing a deeper kind of happiness, a state of psychological well-being whose elements include:

- Having a strong sense of meaning in life
- Being engaged with your life
- Making good use of your strengths
- Functioning at your best
- Serving a purpose beyond yourself
- Realizing your potential (also known as self-actualization)

A practical definition of eudaimonic well-being is that it is the experience of fulfilment that results when someone acts in accordance with their own source of meaning. It is also a form of spiritual well-being which comes about through transcendence, being motivated by something that is beyond the self. For some people this may mean a personal spiritual pathway but you may also feel you want to make a difference in the wider community, such as by:

- Pursuing a vocation or calling in life
- Helping to raise the next generation
- Supporting a community
- Contributing to a cause you're passionate about

Many people who have come through trauma feel motivated to work with others to achieve positive change in the world. It is the inspiration behind many charities – making something good come out of adversity. Having been the target of cyberstalking, what empowered me was the idea that my experience could help others. Our sepsis survivor got involved with a patient group at the hospital where his amputations were carried out. 'I've had the opportunity to talk with patients who are facing a similar situation in order to offer hope to them in what are clearly difficult times. My wife and I have also joined a choir set up to raise funds for a device to help patients who are unable to talk and communicate with staff. I was unable to talk for a week when I came out of my coma and know how difficult that is to deal with.'

So a vital personal question is: what is truly meaningful to you now that you'd be prepared to dedicate your efforts toward?

How can you perform the alchemy that can make something good out of something that was so painful? What ripple can you send out into the world as a positive legacy from the traumatic events you have lived through?

One of the benefits of eudaimonic well-being is that it is longer-lasting and more sustainable than the short-term happiness of hedonic well-being, which comes from the pursuit of pleasure.

And finally

Together we have been on a journey through adversity and now we have come out the other end in a place of growth. Whether you've just experienced a trauma yourself, think someone close to you might be experiencing PTS or are starting to feel more resilient after a period of feeling lost and overwhelmed, learning about the phenomenon of PTG can be a turning point.

I hope that this book has been a source of comfort for you, helping to guide you through to recovery and increasing your chances of finding ways to transform trauma into growth. As one of the people in the case studies puts it, 'I wouldn't change what happened or my life for the world; this experience has made me a stronger person and happy in my own shoes.'

What next?

I have a coaster on my desk that reads 'Where there's tea, there's hope.' A cup of tea has certainly sustained me through many a difficult moment as well as through the writing of this book. My hope is that learning about post-traumatic growth will be a game-changer for you, assuring you that things *can* change, that there is light at the end of the tunnel, and that there is reason to be hopeful about the possibilities for the future.

To this end I have suggested some further reading and useful websites in the following pages, which will allow you to explore PTG further.

'Look on the bright side' is a piece of advice that is often dished out but will sound hollow and somewhat alien to anyone who is going through adversity. While there is no doubt that optimism has significant benefits for your psychological and physical well-being, understandably it can be difficult to think optimistically when your life is in pieces. That's why I like the scientific conceptualization of hope, something that post-traumatic growth can offer you when you're ready – a practical pathway to positive change.

One approach to hope that I find helpful is breaking it down into three practical steps, so when you're ready you might like to try the following:

- Identify what you would ideally like in life (the goal)
- Think of a variety of routes toward this goal (pathways)
- Apply yourself with motivation and energy along these pathways to achieve the goal (agency)

Taking action like this is fundamental in moving forward after trauma. I know from my years of experience in the field of positive psychology that there is only so far you can get with *reading* about the subject. The change will only ever come with putting the knowledge into *action*. Happiness is not a spectator sport; it is the practice of techniques like the ones outlined in this book that forms the neural pathways to make a habit out of happiness. My hope is that the content of this book will give you hope that you are not alone, inspiration that you will get through tough times, and knowledge and tools to help you rebuild your life from the inside out. Where there is a will there will almost certainly be a way.

Further reading

I recommend these books to continue your exploration of the journey from PTS to PTG.

Akhtar, Miriam, *Positive Psychology for Overcoming Depression*, Watkins, 2012

Bannink, Fredrike, *Post Traumatic Success*, Norton, 2014

Boniwell, Ilona, *Positive Psychology in a Nutshell*, PWBC, 2006

Calhoun, Lawrence, and Richard Tedeschi, *Posttraumatic Growth in Clinical Practice*, Routledge, 2013

Craig, Gary, *EFT for PTSD*, Energy Psychology Press, 2009

Dweck, Carol, *Mindset: How You Can Fulfil Your Potential*, Random House, 2006

Frankl, Viktor, *Man's Search for Meaning*, Beacon Press, 2006

Fredrickson, Barbara, *Positivity*, Crown, 2009

Gottman, John, and Nan Silver, *The Seven Principles for Making Marriage Work*, Three Rivers Press, 1999

Hefferon, Kate, and Ilona Boniwell, *Positive Psychology: Theory, Research and Applications*, Open University, 2011

Johnstone, Chris, *Find Your Power: A Toolkit for Resilience and Positive Change*, 2nd edn, Permanent Publications, 2010

Ivtzan, Itai, Tim Lomas, Kate Hefferon, Piers Worth, *Second Wave Positive Psychology*, Routledge, 2016

Joseph, Stephen, *What Doesn't Kill Us*, Piatkus, 2011

Lal, Tara, *Standing on my Brother's Shoulders*, Watkins, 2015

Reivich, Karen, and Andrew Shatté, *The Resilience Factor*, Broadway Books, 2003

Rendon, Jim, *Upside*, Touchstone Press, 2015

Rothschild, Babette, *The Body Remembers: The Psychophysiology of Trauma and Trauma Treatment*, Norton, 2000

Seligman, Martin, *Learned Optimism*, Alfred A Knopf, 1990

Seligman, Martin, *Flourish*, Nicholas Brealey Publishing, 2011

Shapiro, Francine, *Getting Past Your Past: Take Control of Your Life with Self-Help Techniques from EMDR Therapy*, Rodale, 2013

van der Kolk, Bessel, *The Body Keeps the Score*, Penguin, 2015

Ware, Bronnie, *The Top 5 Regrets of the Dying*, Hay House UK, 2012

Williams, Mark, John Teasdale, Zindel Segal, Jon Kabat-Zinn, *The Mindful Way Through Depression*, Guilford Press, 2007

Useful websites

The major research bodies studying PTG include the following:

The Post Traumatic Growth Research Unit at the University of East London:
    www.uel.ac.uk/Schools/Psychology/Research/Health-Promotion-and-Behaviour/Post-Traumatic-Growth

The PTG research group at the University of North Carolina where Tedeschi and Calhoun, the originators of PTG, are based:
    https://ptgi.uncc.edu

The Centre for Trauma, Resilience and Growth:
    www.nottinghamshirehealthcare.nhs.uk/centre-for-trauma-resilience-growth

Other useful websites providing a variety of resources and additional information are:

University of Pennsylvania's positive psychology website:
    www.authentichappiness.sas.upenn.edu

Penny Brohn UK. Living well with cancer: www.pennybrohn.org.uk

MIND: www.mind.org.uk

HelpGuide: www.helpguide.org

Web-MD: www.webmd.com

Diagnostic and Statistical Manual, 5th edition: www.dsm5.org

National Center for PTSD: www.ptsd.va.gov

PTSD UK: www.ptsduk.org

Black Dog Institute: www.blackdoginstitute.org.au

Green Exercise Research Group, University of Essex:
    www.greenexercise.org

The Greater Good Science Center, University of California: www.greatergood.berkeley.edu

Dr Andrew Weil demonstrating the 4–7–8 breath: www.drweil.com/videos-features/videos/breathing-exercises-4-7-8-breath

EMDR Institute: www.emdr.com

EFT founder Gary Craig's website: www.emofree.com

Center for Mindfulness in Medicine: www.umassmed.edu/cfm

The Trauma Center, founded by Dr Bessel van der Kolk: www.traumacenter.org

International Society for Neurofeedback and Research (ISNR): www.isnr.org

You can download a complete set of references from my website: www.positivepsychologytraining.co.uk

Acknowledgments

I'd like to express my gratitude to all those who kindly gave their stories to the book. Thanks to Prof. Stephen Joseph and Dr Kate Hefferon, both PTG experts, who generously shared their knowledge. I'd also like to thank Dr Chris Johnstone, Felicity Biggart, Ashley Akin-Smith, Dr Catherine Zollman, Tara Lal, Sarah Bird, Josie Jacobs, Carlos Ferreira, Camilla Lovelace, Antonia Sigtryggsdottir, David Carson, Will Glennon, Simon Barnes of Be Mindful, Prof. Neil Frude, Prof. Helena Marujo, Prof. Luis Miguel Neto, Dr Evgeny Osin, Kate Johnstone, Jen Gash, Maggie Jeffery, Byron Lee, Chris Samsa, Anastasia Cambitzi, Rosalind Turner, Miranda Steed and Shona Harris. Thank you Kelly Thompson and Watkins Media for understanding the value of post-traumatic growth and sending the knowledge of it out into the world. And thank you to my wonderful community of friends and colleagues who fed my reservoir of resilience while writing this book.

ABOUT THE AUTHOR

MIRIAM AKHTAR

Miriam Akhtar is one of the UK's leading positive psychology practitioners and authors, and is one of 100 global experts invited to contribute to *The World Book of Happiness*. She is the author of four previous books, including *Positive Psychology for Overcoming Depression* for Watkins. She is also a coach, consultant, keynote speaker and visiting lecturer at a number of universities on MAPP (MSc Applied Positive Psychology) programmes. For more information, visit: www.positivepsychologytraining.co.uk

ABOUT THE SERIES

We hope you've enjoyed reading this book.
If you'd like to find out more about other therapies, practices
and phenomena that you've heard of and been curious about,
then do take a look at the other titles in our thought-provoking
#WHATIS series by visiting www.whatisseries.com

#WHATIS

The growing list of dynamic books in this series will allow
you to explore a wide range of life-enhancing topics – sharing
the history, wisdom and science of each subject, as well as
its far-reaching practical applications and benefits. With each guide
written by a practising expert in the field, this new series challenges
preconceptions, demystifies the subjects in hand and encourages
you to find new ways to lead a more fulfilled, meaningful and
contented life.

OTHER TITLES IN THE **#WHATIS** SERIES:

What is a Near-Death Experience? by Dr Penny Sartori
What is Sound Healing? by Lyz Cooper
What is Hypnosis? by Tom Fortes Mayer
What is Numerology? by Sonia Ducie
What is Mindfulness? by Dr Tamara Russell

WATKINS

Sharing Wisdom Since
1893

The story of Watkins dates back to 1893, when the scholar of esotericism John Watkins founded a bookshop, inspired by the lament of his friend and teacher Madame Blavatsky that there was nowhere in London to buy books on mysticism, occultism or metaphysics. That moment marked the birth of Watkins, soon to become the home of many of the leading lights of spiritual literature, including Carl Jung, Rudolf Steiner, Alice Bailey and Chögyam Trungpa.

Today, the passion at Watkins Publishing for vigorous questioning is still resolute. Our wide-ranging and stimulating list reflects the development of spiritual thinking and new science over the past 120 years. We remain at the cutting edge, committed to publishing books that change lives.

DISCOVER MORE . . .

Read our blog

Watch and listen to
our authors in action

Sign up to
our mailing list

JOIN IN THE CONVERSATION

 WatkinsPublishing   @watkinswisdom

watkinsbooks   watkinswisdom   watkins-media

Our books celebrate conscious, passionate, wise and happy living.
Be part of the community by visiting

www.watkinspublishing.com

S0-AET-346

A BAD CASE OF
GHOSTS

J FIC Oppel

Oppel, K.
A bad case of ghosts.

MAR 02 2010

PRICE: $6.99 (3559/he   )

ALSO BY KENNETH OPPEL

Starclimber

Skybreaker

Airborn

Darkwing

Firewing

Sunwing

Silverwing

Dead Water Zone

The Live-Forever Machine

(For Younger Readers)

The King's Taster

Peg and the Yeti

Peg and the Whale

Emma's Emu

A Strange Case of Magic

A Crazy Case of Robots

An Incredible Case of Dinosaurs

A Weird Case of Super-Goo

A Creepy Case of Vampires

KENNETH OPPEL

BARNES & THE BRAINS

A BAD CASE OF
GHOSTS

Harper*Trophy*Canada™
An imprint of HarperCollins Publishers Ltd

A Bad Case of Ghosts
Copyright © 1994, 2000 by Firewing Productions Inc.
All rights reserved.

Published by Harper*Trophy*Canada™, an imprint of HarperCollins Publishers Ltd
Originally published in Canada by Scholastic Canada Ltd: 1994
This Harper*Trophy*Canada™ edition: 2010

No part of this book may be used or reproduced in any manner whatsoever
without the prior written permission of the publisher, except in the case of
brief quotations embodied in reviews.

Harper*Trophy*Canada™ is a trademark
of HarperCollins Publishers

HarperCollins books may be purchased for educational, business,
or sales promotional use through our Special Markets Department.

HarperCollins Publishers Ltd
2 Bloor Street East, 20th Floor
Toronto, Ontario, Canada
M4W 1A8

www.harpercollins.ca

Library and Archives Canada Cataloguing in Publication
information is available upon request

ISBN 978-1-55468-528-8

Illustrations by Victor Rivas Villa
Printed and bound in Canada
DWF 9 8 7 6 5 4 3 2 1

FSC
Mixed Sources
Cert no. SW-COC-001271
© 1996 FSC

for Lloyd

Contents

Chapter 1

Spooked

Giles Barnes couldn't sleep.

He sat up in bed, hugging a pillow to his chest, and looked around the dark room. There was hardly anything in it. The moving van had arrived very late and there hadn't been much time to unpack. Apart from his bed, the only other things in the room were cardboard crates and bits of furniture pushed against the walls. Pale light from the street seeped through the grimy window and cast weird, dinosaur-shaped shadows across the empty room.

He didn't like this new house of theirs. From the moment he'd set foot inside, he felt there was something dark and sad about it. Plaster was flaking off the ceilings in big patches, the wallpaper was droopy, the doors hung

1

crookedly on their hinges, and the creaky wood floors had splinters in them. There was a funny smell to the house, too, which reminded him of his Grandma's root cellar, dark and unfriendly.

"It's a great old house," his father had said enthusiastically when they arrived. "It's just been shut tight for a long time. All it needs is a good airing out. And a little fixing up."

"And a *lot* of fixing up," said his mother, showing him the doorknob which had just pulled off in her hand.

"I wish we were back in our old place," Giles grumbled to himself in bed. He'd had to say good-bye to Jim and David, his best friends, and now there was a whole summer to get through without knowing anyone. He didn't understand why they'd had to move at all. What was wrong with their old house? It was a lot better than this ancient thing—he'd be surprised if it didn't fall to pieces before the end of the week!

A shadow shaped like a Triceratops moved across the wall and Giles shuddered. It's just a car going by outside, he told himself. You have an overactive imagination. Mom's always saying so.

But a sudden creak sent a little ripple of electricity up and down his neck.

"It's just the floors," he told himself, trying to sound sensible like his mother. "Old houses make lots of strange noises. There's nothing to be afraid of."

The radiator clanked and Giles jumped.

"This is ridiculous," he said. "I'm going to sleep."

But his eyes were closed for only a few seconds before he heard a strange, rustling sound in the room. He popped open his eyes. It was coming from the corner by the window. No, it was closer to the door . . . no, it was up near the ceiling, then away to the right of the bed. This weird, whispery fluttering noise seemed to be moving!

Giles was starting to get freaked out. He'd had it with moving shadows and strange noises. He jumped out of bed and switched on the light. The noise stopped. All the monstrous shadows evaporated. It was just like his mother was always telling him. Turn on the lights, the noises always stop. Giles took a good look around his room, then flicked off the light, dived back into bed, and pulled the covers up to his ears.

There was some more creaking, but he didn't let it bother him. Besides, he was getting too drowsy to care anymore. Soon he was fast asleep.

Chapter 2

The Quarks

The next morning, Giles started unpacking his things. First he set up his desk and shelves. That helped—already the room was beginning to look a little nicer, more like home. He wasn't crazy about the wallpaper, which was a dingy, greyish colour with a faded pattern of vines and ivy leaves. He stuck up some of his favourite posters with putty.

The window was so dirty he could barely see out. He asked Dad for a cloth and some cleaning liquid and gave the glass a good scrub. It was a sunny summer day, and there were lots of people on the sidewalks. He could see an old man, leaning on a walker, making his way slowly past their house.

Across the street was a small park. Giles squinted. Weird!

Perched on the monkey bars were a boy and a girl. That wasn't weird. It was what they were wearing. They both wore enormous sets of headphones which were plugged into a large machine which the girl carried around her neck on a thick strap. And they were both looking straight at his house!

As Giles watched, the girl twiddled a few knobs on the machine and then said something to the boy. They climbed down from the monkey bars, crossed the street and stood on the sidewalk, staring intently at the house.

Giles could see them more clearly now. He guessed that they were about his age. The girl was very tiny, with small, thin hands, pale skin, and two precise blond braids dangling on either side of her head. The boy had tightly curled red hair, and his broad face was splotched with freckles.

But what were they *doing* with that machine?

The girl said something to the boy, but he obviously didn't hear her. She knocked on his head with her knuckles to get his attention. They had a short conversation.

Then, as Giles watched in amazement, they actually walked through the front gate of the house and into the garden! They stood on the lawn, listening to their headphones again, and the girl was now scribbling in a notepad.

What on earth?

Giles couldn't control his curiosity any longer. He went downstairs, opened the front door and walked out. The boy and girl didn't seem to notice him.

"Hello," he said uncertainly.

No response.

"Hey," he said, more loudly.

They both jumped, and yanked off their headphones.

"Hi," said the boy with the red hair. "Do you live here?"

"We just moved in," Giles told him.

The boy and girl looked at each other in surprise.

"Oh," said the boy. "We thought it was still empty. I'm Kevin Quark, and this is my older sister, Tina. We're geniuses."

Giles blinked.

"Kevin," said the tiny girl, "shut up."

"Well, it's true isn't it?"

"Of course, but it's not the kind of thing you tell people when you first meet them, is it?"

8

Kevin smiled cheerfully. "Oh well," he said. "So, what's your name?"

"Giles Barnes."

"Are you a genius?"

"I've never really thought about it," Giles replied.

"Well, it's usually pretty obvious," Kevin told him. "Can you name all the capital cities of Europe? Do you get ten out of ten on all your class quizzes? Can you do the thirteen-times table in your head? Those are some of the first signs."

Giles felt out of breath just listening to Kevin.

"We've counted the number of bricks in our house, and calculated the amount of water that flushes through the toilet every day. Sometimes we invent things—Tina's brilliant at that. She knows everything about chemistry and electricity. She can make liquid in a test tube turn blue and then explode! She can make sparks sizzle between two rods!"

Tina stood there silently, smiling faintly.

"Well, I don't think I'm genius material, compared with all that," Giles admitted.

"Well, that's all right," said Kevin good-naturedly,

"I'm only a little bit of a genius myself. Now, Tina, she's a vast genius. She's the brains behind the whole operation. The ghostometer was her idea."

Tina nudged her brother in the ribs with her elbow.

"Owww!" Kevin cried out. "What was that for?"

"For telling him about the ghostometer."

"The what?" Giles said.

Tina sighed. "The ghostometer," she said. "It detects ghosts."

Giles took a good look at the contraption around her neck. It looked like a toaster with lots of switches and knobs added on.

"That thing detects ghosts?" he said. "You're not serious!"

"I'm completely serious," said the tiny girl. "I'll admit, it does need some minor re-adjustments. But I'll have you know that we got some very strong readings from your house."

"Did we?" Kevin asked.

Tina rolled her eyes. "Yes, Kevin, we did. Weren't you listening?"

"Sometimes it all sounds the same to me. All those little beeps and blerps."

11

"They were positive readings," Tina said, exasperated.

"But didn't we get positive readings from Tom's dog once?" Kevin asked politely.

Tina went red in the face. "Yes, that was in the early stages. It's much more reliable now."

"Hang on a second," said Giles. "You think my house is haunted?"

"It's possible," said Tina gravely.

"I don't believe in ghosts," Giles said firmly, trying to sound like his mother.

"Are you sure you haven't seen anything spooky or creepy or basically weird in there?" Kevin wanted to know.

"No," said Giles quickly, "absolutely not."

He couldn't help thinking about the strange noises he'd heard in his room last night. But that was just his imagination. It had nothing whatsoever to do with ghosts.

"Well," said Kevin eagerly, "no one's lived in this house for years. I bet it's haunted. They say a crazy lady used to live there. She never left the house. There's bound to be ghosts coming out of every nook and cranny!"

"Kevin, please," said Tina in a tired voice, "this is all very unscientific. We haven't proven anything yet."

Giles took a look at his house. Now that he thought about it, it *did* look a little haunted. He felt a tingling at the base of his skull. Had a crazy lady really lived here? Could there really be ghosts?

"Well, look," said Tina, "we've got to do some work on the ghostometer."

"And if anything zany happens," said Kevin hopefully, "give us a call and we'll be right over. Here's our card."

"Good-bye," said Giles, feeling slightly over-whelmed. He looked at the business card Kevin put in his hand. It said:

Tina and Kevin Quark.
Local Geniuses.
Capable of just about everything.
Reasonable Rates.

"I've never met geniuses before," Giles mumbled, going inside.

Chapter 3

Haunted

"I met some kids who said this house is haunted," Giles told his parents at lunch.

"There's no such thing as ghosts," Mrs Barnes said with a smile. Mrs Barnes was a professor of mathematics at the university. She liked numbers, she liked long equations, she liked things you could solve on paper. She did not believe in ghosts.

"Aunt Lillian believes in ghosts," Giles pointed out.

"Yes, well, Aunt Lillian believes in quite a few odd things," said Mrs Barnes.

Giles liked Aunt Lillian, no matter what his Mom said. Aunt Lillian dressed like a gypsy with scarves and headbands, and wore too much makeup. She always told ghost stories when she came.

"Dad, do you believe in ghosts?" Giles asked.

"Well, I'm not sure," said his father. "I've certainly never seen a ghost."

"There you go," said Mrs Barnes. "No one I know has ever seen a ghost. That's because they're not real."

"But there's lots of things we haven't seen which we know are real," said Giles.

"Like what?" Mrs Barnes asked.

"Like . . . like atoms!" said Giles.

"Ah, well, that's different," said Mrs Barnes. "That's science."

"They said a crazy woman used to live here."

"Oh, please," said Mrs Barnes.

"Don't you like the house, Giles?" his father asked.

"It's a little creepy," said Giles.

"It's just an old house, that's all," said Mr Barnes. "Once we get it all fixed up, you won't think it's so bad."

Giles's father was right. After a few days, he'd almost forgotten about the Quarks and their stories about ghosts and crazy ladies. The house was getting more and more cheerful as they arranged their furniture and brought in plants and put up paintings. Mr Barnes was even giving the house a fresh coat of paint on the outside, and he promised to get new wallpaper for Giles's bedroom.

"This house isn't so bad after all," Giles said to himself. He was in his bedroom, working on a model airplane. The sun and the smell of summer were streaming through his window and he was just about to glue a particularly delicate bit of his model together—when he heard it.

He put down his model and listened. There it was again, slightly louder now, that same whispery rustle he'd heard the very first night! He held his breath. If he didn't know any better, he'd have said it sounded like a bird flapping its wings.

It was bright daylight, and Giles didn't feel very frightened at all; in fact, he felt curious. He stood up and walked to his window. Poking out his head, he peered under the eaves. In their old house, some birds had built their nests there, and he'd been able to hear them fluttering around under the roof. But there was nothing to see here, no birds, no nests.

He ducked his head back through the window. He could still hear it! How bizarre. It sounded almost as if a bird was soaring around his bedroom, because the sound was definitely moving, swooping from one corner of his room to the next. But he couldn't see anything!

Now Giles was starting to get nervous. He was all alone in the house. His parents had gone downtown to see about some curtains and wouldn't be home for at least an hour.

Stay calm, he told himself. There must be a perfectly reasonable explanation for all this. What would Mom do if she were here?

Then, all of a sudden—

"Hello!"

The hair at the back of Giles's neck lit up. It was a woman's voice, and it had come from right beside his ear! But there was nothing to be seen!

"Hello, hello!"

That did it! He lunged for his desk and rummaged frantically through his drawers until he found Kevin Quark's business card. Then he slammed the bedroom door behind him, raced to the downstairs phone and punched in the number with a shaking finger.

"Kevin and Tina Quark, local geniuses. May I help you?"

"Kevin," said Giles, recognizing the voice at the other end of the line, "it's Giles Barnes. You'd better come over right away. We've got ghosts!"

Chapter 4

A Bad Case of Ghosts

"I've made some adjustments to the ghostometer," Tina told Giles. "I believe I've perfected it."

"She was up all last night working on it," said Kevin proudly. "She had to take apart the stereo for spare parts."

"Mom and Dad don't know yet," said Tina.

"Oh yes they do," said Kevin. "Mom tried to play one of her Beatles CDs and it sounded like chipmunks."

"It can't be helped," said Tina. "This is important."

"Well, I hope you can figure this one out," said Giles, who'd been waiting for them outside in the front yard. "I was scared half to death."

"Oh boy!" said Kevin. "Ghosts!"

"Kevin," said Tina, "shut up. Now, Barnes, where did you see the ghosts?"

19

"You can call me Giles, you know."

"I prefer Barnes. Now, about the ghosts?"

"Well, I didn't exactly *see* them," Giles said. "I *heard* them. It was this weird fluttering sound, like birds' wings. And then I heard a voice, a woman's voice, say Hello."

"A voice said Hello?" Kevin asked. "That's all?"

"Yes."

"Oh," said Kevin disappointedly. "Doesn't sound very ghostly to me. No skeletons? No people without heads? No gushing—"

"Where did you hear these sounds?" Tina interrupted, giving her brother a withering look.

"In my bedroom." He told them how he'd heard the same sort of noise the very first night he'd arrived.

"Let us begin our investigation there then," said Tina. "Lead the way."

Upstairs, they all stood very still and listened carefully.

"I don't hear a thing," said Kevin. "Are you sure you aren't making this up?"

"It was clear as anything!" Giles protested. "I heard it. It's not my fault if it's gone away now!"

"I am now going to take some readings with the ghos-tometer," Tina announced importantly.

She pulled the headphones over her ears and twirled some knobs. She listened intently for almost a minute, making little noises.

"Ahhhhh," she said, "hmmmmm...uh-huh...ohhhhh."

She took off the headphones and scribbled into a notebook.

"Well?" Giles demanded.

"Very interesting," said Tina.

"Aren't you going to tell us what you heard?" Kevin said.

"No."

"Why not?" blustered Giles.

"I need more information. It would be unprofessional of me to offer an analysis at this early stage."

Tina put the headphones back on and walked slowly around the room.

"She's awfully serious," Giles whispered to Kevin.

"She's a genius," Kevin whispered back. "Geniuses are supposed to be serious. It's a serious business. I'm serious sometimes, too, but since I'm only a little bit of a genius, I don't have to be as serious as Tina."

"I still think that thing looks like a toaster," Giles muttered, nodding at the ghostometer. "I bet it doesn't even work."

"Fascinating," Tina said to herself, jotting more notes into the book.

"Can we listen now?" Kevin inquired.

"No."

"Why not?" Giles demanded.

But Tina didn't say anything. It was as if she were in a trance. Finally she pulled off her headphones and held them out to Kevin and Giles without saying a word. They clunked heads and shared the headphones.

Giles gasped. It wasn't just a simple fluttering of wings he heard this time, it was a *symphony* of bird sounds, chirping and whistling, cooing and squawking, hooting and warbling! And on top of all that was the clatter of beating wings! It was deafening. There must have been dozens of birds making all that racket!

Giles yanked off the headphones.

"Wow!" said Kevin.

"You mean all that's coming from my room!" Giles demanded, looking at Tina.

She was sitting silently on the edge of the bed, her hands folded neatly in her lap.

"Do you believe in ghosts?" she asked.

"I . . . I don't know," Giles stammered. "My mother says they don't exist. But my Aunt Lillian believes in them. She says that—"

"Your room is *haunted*, Barnes," Tina said simply. "The readings on my ghostometer are unmistakable. You've got ghosts. You've got ghosts badly. It's the worst case of ghosts I've ever seen."

"It's also the *first* case of ghosts I've ever seen," Kevin added.

"But who's ever heard of ghost *birds*!" Giles blustered. "I mean—"

But he stopped suddenly. He stared. He pointed.

In the far corner of the room, on top of his bookshelves, was a large parrot. But it wasn't a real parrot. It was shimmering like a heat mirage. It was all silver and glittering, as if someone had drawn it in the air with sparklers. It strutted regally back and forth across the shelf, passing right through some of Giles's model planes.

Giles looked over at Tina, to make sure she was see-ing it, too. She must have been. Her eyes were wide open. Kevin saw it, too. His mouth was wide open, but no words were coming out.

"It's . . . a ghost bird," Giles said.

"A ghost parrot to be precise," said Tina.

"Hello!" said the parrot in a woman's voice. "Hello, hello!"

"Ah-ha!" said Tina. "That explains the voice you heard."

And then, before Giles had time to speak, his entire bedroom was suddenly filled with ghost birds, all gleam-ing white, perched on the furniture, scratching on the desk, strutting around on the window sill; there were birds chirping and singing and flying through the air. One swooped low towards Giles and he ducked, cover-ing his head with his hands. The ghost bird soared right through him, but Giles didn't feel a thing, except a little buzz of static electricity in his head.

"The ghostometer readings are higher than ever before!" shouted Tina above the din.

"This is crazy!" shouted Giles. "My room is filled with ghost birds!"

"Can we go home now?" Kevin asked in a quavering voice.

Just as quickly as they'd come, all the ghost birds suddenly disappeared, and Giles's bedroom was back to normal. Except for a single silvery feather which floated slowly to the floor and stayed there for a moment before dissolving into empty air.

"It's extraordinary," said Tina. "I believe I counted over fifty different specimens."

"You actually counted them?" said Kevin in disbelief. "Weren't you afraid?"

"Fear is unscientific," said Tina.

"That's what my mother would say," said Giles miserably. "What am I going to tell my parents! They won't believe me. They'll think I've flipped!"

"Maybe you'd better let me have a chat with them," said Tina solemnly. "They might listen to me."

Chapter 5

On the Case

"It's a pleasure to make your acquaintance, Mr and Mrs Barnes," said Tina Quark.

"Thank you, Tina," said Giles's father.

Giles saw that his parents were both smiling a little. They couldn't believe that such a tiny girl could be so serious. When Mr and Mrs Barnes had come home from shopping, Tina had asked them to please sit down at the dining room table.

"Now then," said Tina. "I realize that what I am going to tell you may be difficult to believe. But please try to keep an open mind. I have recently made an examination of your house and I've come to the conclusion that you have ghosts."

"I see," said Mr Barnes. "Would anyone like a drink?"

"How have you found this out, Tina?" Mrs Barnes asked.

"With the ghostometer," Kevin blurted out.

Tina shot her younger brother an incinerating glare. "Kevin, please, allow me to do the explaining here."

She lifted the ghostometer onto the table and showed it to Giles's parents.

"Mr and Mrs Barnes, this is a ghostometer, a personal invention of mine. It measures the amount of ghost activity which human beings can't normally detect."

"It looks like a toaster," mumbled Mr Barnes.

Tina pretended she didn't hear that.

"With this device I have discovered a very high concentration of ghost activity in your son's bedroom."

"It's true," Giles told his parents. "We all saw them when you and Mom were out. We saw ghosts!"

"Now look," said Mrs Barnes, getting into her stern professor mood, "I'm a woman of science myself, Tina, and I must tell you that what you're saying is preposterous, not to mention totally unscientific . . ."

As Mrs Barnes was speaking, Giles caught sight of something moving. He squinted. One of the ghost birds was swooping into the dining room from the hallway. It was the same regal parrot which Giles had seen in his bedroom.

"Um, Mom," said Giles, "there's—"

"Giles, please, let me finish," said his mother. "Now, never have I read a scientific account of ghosts which I have found satisfactory . . ."

The ghost parrot fluttered through the room and perched on Mrs Barnes's shoulder. Giles saw it. So did Kevin and Tina. So did Mr Barnes. Mrs Barnes, however, was too busy talking to take notice.

"Um, Mom," said Giles again.

"Giles, now let me—*ahgggg*!" screamed Mrs Barnes, finally seeing the bird on her shoulder. "Where the heck did that come from?"

"It's what I've been trying to tell you, Mrs Barnes," said Tina patiently. "You've got a bad case of ghosts— ghost birds to be precise."

Mrs Barnes was trying to shoo the ghost bird off her shoulder, but her hand just went right through with a little buzzing sound.

"Well, Liz," said Mr Barnes to his wife in a dazed voice, "it looks like Aunt Lillian was right."

"This is some kind of trick, isn't it!" Mrs Barnes exclaimed. "All right, very funny, game's over."

"Mom, it's a real ghost!" Giles insisted. "There's dozens of them in my room. This house is haunted!"

Mrs Barnes had her neck craned as far away from her shoulder as possible. She was staring into the eyes of the ghost bird, and the ghost bird was staring right back.

"Hello, hello!" said the parrot.

"There seems to be a parrot on my shoulder," she mumbled to herself.

"Where do they come from?" Mr Barnes asked.

"Impossible to say," Tina replied calmly. "I'd have to research such a question very thoroughly before I could supply you with an adequate answer."

"Well, look," said Mr Barnes. "This is completely unacceptable. We can't have ghost birds flying around our house. How can we get rid of them?"

"Another very good question, Mr Barnes," said Tina. "Let me assure you that we'll get to work on it right away. In the meantime, I don't think there's any danger."

"Easy for you to say!" said Giles. "You don't have to

sleep in my room! It's like an airport in there, all those birds swooping around my head!"

"Don't worry, we'll figure it out," said Kevin confidently. "After all, we are geniuses."

Chapter 6

Ghost Overload

"There's birds in the bathroom now!" blustered Mrs Barnes.

"Just try to ignore them," Mr Barnes suggested. "They're perfectly harmless."

"There's no privacy in this house any more!" Mrs Barnes grumbled.

Giles couldn't help smiling. In the past two days, the ghost birds had taken over the entire house. They appeared and vanished without warning, sometimes one or two, sometimes dozens at a time. Most of them did seem to prefer Giles's bedroom, but it was not at all uncommon for a ghost cockatoo or a ghost budgie to turn up in the living room and roost on the television, or perch on a towel rack in the bathroom.

The regal ghost parrot seemed to have taken a special liking to Giles's mother and would often settle affectionately on her shoulder during meals, or as she walked around the house.

"What a ridiculous creature," Mrs Barnes would mutter, trying to shoo it away without success. "Won't this thing leave me alone!"

Giles's mother was not taking the ghostly invasion well at all. Giles knew that it was very hard for his scientific mother to admit that there really were ghosts living in their house and nibbling at her earlobes.

"We're not telling anyone about this," she instructed them. "I'd be the laughing stock of the mathematics department. Ghost birds! Hah!"

"Can't we even tell Aunt Lillian?" Giles wanted to know. "She'd be thrilled to see ghost birds."

"Absolutely not," said Mrs Barnes. "She'd tell everyone she knew. She'd call the papers. We'd be on the nine o'clock news. No. We tell no one."

As for Giles, he found he was gradually getting used to the ghost birds. He thought they were sort of beautiful, these sleek, silvery things, glittering with mysterious light. A few days later he discovered that you could make them disappear by blowing on them. They would flicker like a candle flame and then dissolve. But it was only temporary and after a few minutes, they would come back.

Often he could ignore the ghost birds altogether, but that wasn't always possible when they filled his room as if it were some giant cage, shrieking and chirping and beating their wings. He'd started wearing ear-plugs in bed at night so he wouldn't be woken up by their early morning racket.

"When are we going to get rid of these things?" his mother roared that evening at the dinner table, puffing at every ghost bird that fluttered into view.

"Tina and Kevin are working on something," Giles said.

"They *are* geniuses," Mr Barnes reminded his wife.

"Geniuses, right!" said Giles's mother. "I just hope they manage to clear these birds out of our house before I go crazy!"

Later that evening, Giles was sitting up in bed, trying to read. A finch flew over and perched on the top of his book. Giles blew on it and it disappeared. He read

35

another sentence and then an African swallow dive-bombed him.

"Hello, hello!" said the parrot, who suddenly decided to put in an appearance.

Giles lay his book down with a sigh. His room was overrun once again. Where did they all come from? He hoped that Kevin and Tina cooked up something fast. He wasn't sure how much more of this he could take!

All at once, Giles was aware of something else in the room with him.

Not a bird this time.

It was a person.

He turned his head to look. In the far corner of the room was an elderly woman. But, of course, she wasn't really a woman at all. She was all crackling light and electricity, just like the birds!

Giles sat rigidly in bed, watching her. It was one thing to see ghost birds, quite another to see the ghost of a real human being! Giles was certain the hair on his head was slowly rising. Was this the crazy lady Kevin had talked about?

But the ghost woman didn't take any notice of him at all. She moved across the room, half walking, half gliding. She was looking carefully at the birds, stroking their plumage. She seemed upset, and Giles immediately felt sorry for her. She went from bird to bird, gazing at each one anxiously.

Then she turned and looked straight at Giles.

Giles felt his whole body go limp with fear. What's she going to do now? Giles wondered. All sorts of gory images flashed before his mind's eye. But the ghost woman just shook her head sadly. She had a kind face, with plenty of wrinkles, and silvery hair gathered on top of her head in a bun.

She raised a ghostly silver hand and pointed to the ceiling of Giles's bedroom. Then, taking one last look at the birds, she slowly faded from view until there was nothing left of her except a sprinkling of light hanging in the air, and that too disappeared after a moment.

First ghost birds, Giles thought, now a ghost woman. What did it all mean?

Chapter 7

The Attic

"You mean there's another ghost now?" Kevin exclaimed. "I think we're into ghost overload!"

"I haven't told my Mom," said Giles. "She's getting pretty grumpy about the birds as it is. The strange thing is, the birds *love* her. There's a budgie that's been nesting on top of her head lately. It makes her furious. If I told her there was the ghost of an old woman walking around, she'd go completely over the edge!"

"I bet it's the crazy lady everyone was talking about!" Kevin said enthusiastically. "Did she look crazy?"

"No, she didn't," said Giles. "She looked sad."

"Oh," said Kevin, disappointed.

Giles was trying to find a place to sit down in Tina

and Kevin Quark's basement workshop, which was filled to bursting with old bits and pieces of furniture and machinery. He settled for an upturned cardboard box.

"Dad and I called up Aunt Lillian in secret," he told the two Quarks. "And she said that ghosts are people who were very unhappy or upset when they died, and they keep on being unhappy for a long time afterwards. So they wander around all sad, trying to figure things out."

"But what about all the birds?" said Kevin. "Who's ever heard of sad birds?"

"It's weird, I know," said Giles. "But the old woman's obviously sad. And I think it has something to do with all the birds. They must have belonged to her. Listen to this. Remember how I told you the ghost lady pointed at the ceiling? Well, after I told Dad, I was wondering what it all meant. And I thought maybe she was pointing to the attic!"

"The attic!" said Kevin. "Now this is more like it! Did you go up?"

Giles nodded. "I didn't even know we had an attic. But Dad and I found a trap door in the ceiling. It pulled down with a little set of steps. We got some flashlights and climbed up. It was really dusty. Dad kept sneezing. But we found hundreds of old, empty bird cages in a big pile!"

"Hundreds, Barnes?" said Tina. "That sounds like somewhat of an exaggeration."

Giles rolled his eyes. "All right, not hundreds. But there were *lots*. I didn't count them. But whoever this woman was, she must have had a lot of pet birds."

"Wow," said Kevin.

"Dad called up some of our neighbours, but none of them remembered who used to live in the house before us. Most of the people Dad talked to hadn't lived on the street that long. I wish I knew what happened."

"Yes, well," said Tina, looking up from a new gadget she'd been fiddling with, "I think we can give this a try."

"What is it?" Giles asked.

"It's great," said Kevin. "She took apart practically everything in the house to make it—the radio, TV, electric egg-beater. She's brilliant."

"Kevin—" said Tina.

"I know, I know," sighed her brother, "shut up."

"Exactly. Now then, what I've been working on is a device which should make the ghosts disappear for good. Stand back everyone, please."

She flipped a little switch on the side of the contraption. There was a loud whirring noise, then a coughing, spluttering sound, and a big plume of yellow and black smoke curled up into the air.

"Well," said Tina. "That wasn't a huge success, was it?"

"Tina? Kevin?" a voice called down from the top of the stairs. "What's going on down there?"

"Nothing, Mom," said Tina.

"Don't worry," Kevin said to Giles, fanning smoke away from his face. "We'll come up with something. You won't have to live with ghosts for the rest of your life."

"Maybe we should try to find out more about the woman who used to live there," Giles suggested. "Maybe that would help."

Tina looked doubtful.

"It doesn't sound very scientific," she said.

"But it's a real mystery," Giles said. Something terrible must have happened. But what? If he knew that, maybe he'd be able to free his house from all the ghosts.

Chapter 8

Melanie Jones

On his way home from the Quarks', Giles saw an old man making his way down the street with the help of a walker, leaning heavily on the metal handles. Giles had seen him many times before. Every day at four o'clock he would shuffle very slowly down to the end of Stoker Street, then turn round and go back. It took him about forty-five minutes. But this evening, he stopped right in front of Giles's house.

"Hello," Giles said, walking up to him. "Can I help you?"

He thought at first that the old man might be feeling sick. But now he saw that he was looking intently at the house, gazing straight up at his bedroom window.

"Oh, hello," the old man said, still staring at Giles's

window. "It's silly, isn't it, but I still expect to see birds in there."

Giles's heart thudded. "I'm sorry, what do you mean?" he asked, surprised. Could he know about the ghost birds, too? Had he seen them flying around?

"She used to keep lots of birds, Melanie. She had so many birds she barely knew what to do with them. Kept most of them in that room, right up there. I used to be able to see them when I took my walk."

"Did you know her?" Giles asked hopefully.

"Hardly at all," the man said. "No one really knew her. She barely put a foot out her door. Everyone thought she was a little batty, mind you, with all those birds. Poor Melanie Jones. It was a shame what happened. I only found out years later."

Giles waited patiently for him to continue.

"Bad heart," he said. "Melanie had a bad heart. I think they wanted to get her into one of those homes, but she wouldn't hear of it. She wouldn't have been able to look after those birds. But she had a heart attack one night, and they came and took her to hospital, but she never woke up. And there was no one to look after her birds. They all starved to death, poor things, before anyone thought to look in on them. It was sad, very sad."

"Oh," said Giles quietly. And suddenly everything clicked in his head. The ghost lady was Melanie Jones, coming back to take care of her poor, starved birds!

* * *

"I've just seen a lady ghost walk through the bathroom," said Mrs Barnes, her face pale, as Giles rushed in the front door.

"It's the ghost of Melanie Jones," Giles said excitedly. "She's the one who lived here before us. She's the one who had all the birds!"

"Oh," said Mrs Barnes. She hadn't blinked in quite a while.

"How did you find this out?" Mr Barnes wanted to know.

"The old man with the walker," Giles said, and he repeated the story he'd just heard outside.

"Well, that's just great," blustered Mrs Barnes, who was beginning to recover from her shock. "But enough is enough. This is the last straw. There I was, getting ready for a nice hot shower, without budgies and bluejays, and just as I was about to step in, the ghost of Melanie Jones hustles through!"

"How awful," said Mr Barnes, trying to stifle his laughter.

"There's got to be laws about this kind of thing," muttered Mrs Barnes. "Invasion of privacy by ghosts of various description!"

The adoring ghost parrot chose that moment to settle on Mrs Barnes's shoulder and nuzzle her ear affectionately.

"Hello, hello," it whispered.

Giles gave it a sharp blast of air.

"Awkkk," said the parrot as it disappeared.

"Oh dear," said Mr Barnes. "I have to admit, it's getting a little much. How are we supposed to lead a normal life? What about the Quarks? Have they figured something out?"

"Not yet," said Giles. "The last gadget Tina invented just went up in a puff of smoke."

What he didn't tell them was that he had an inkling of an idea of his own. He didn't want to say anything yet; he wasn't a genius after all. He wanted to think it through. But maybe, just maybe, it would solve all their problems.

Chapter 9

The Plan

"I have a plan," Giles announced the next day.

He'd called up Tina and Kevin and asked them to come right over, and now they were all sitting at the dining room table. His mother and father were there, too. So was the ghost parrot and a squadron of budgies which were circling Mrs Barnes's head and bombing her with ghost bird droppings.

Giles took a deep breath.

"Ghosts are usually very sad because something went wrong when they were alive. That's why they're still here, because they're trying to fix things up. Except that they can't because they're dead. But they can't rest properly until they think everything's OK again."

"Who told you all this?" asked Mrs Barnes.

"Aunt Lillian," Giles admitted.

"I won't listen. I don't believe a word that comes out of her mouth," Mrs Barnes replied.

"That's what you said *before* you had a ghost parrot sitting on your shoulder," Mr Barnes reminded her. "It won't hurt to listen, Elizabeth. Go ahead, Giles."

"Well, Melanie Jones keeps coming back because she's worried about all her birds. She must have loved them more than anything. She had dozens. But when she died they didn't have any food. So she couldn't feed them, and nobody else thought to feed them, so they starved to death."

He paused and looked around the table. Tina was looking at him very seriously.

"Maybe," Giles said, "if we *feed* the ghost birds, Melanie Jones will stop worrying and she won't feel so sad and all the ghosts will go away for good!"

There was a long silence.

"Barnes," Tina said, "do you have any idea how unscientific that sounds?"

"Well . . ." he stammered.

"Those birds aren't real," Tina said. "They're ghosts. How could they *eat* anything?"

"Look," said Giles, "I know it sounds crazy, but it does kind of make sense. There's nothing anybody can do to change what happened, but maybe if we show Melanie Jones and the birds that we care, that'll be enough. Do you have a better idea?"

There was another long pause.

"No, I don't," Tina said. "My last gadget just burst into flames. And I don't think I'm going to be making any more for quite a while. Mom and Dad found out about the radio and the television—"

"And the electric egg-beater, and the frying pan," Kevin added. "Oh, and don't forget the *Encyclopaedia Britannica*. They weren't very pleased about that either."

"Yes, it's been a bit of disaster, really," said Tina, folding her tiny hands on the table. "We may have to shut down our genius business temporarily."

"Well," said Giles, "then we have no choice. We have to try my idea."

"All right," said Tina.

"I think I must be crazy, but I'm willing to try anything," muttered Mrs Barnes, glaring at the parrot on her shoulder. "Let's get started."

Chapter 10

The Big Feed

"We'd like sixty-three pounds of your finest bird seed," said Giles.

"Sixty-three pounds," said the pet shop owner, looking at Giles as if this were all some huge practical joke. "That's an unusual amount of bird seed. Usually we sell these somewhat smaller boxes."

"No, that's not enough," said Tina Quark very seriously. "I've calculated our requirements exactly, and we need sixty-three pounds of bird seed."

"I see," said the pet shop owner, taken aback.

"And some of those birdie treats," said Kevin enthusiastically. "Yeah, they'll love those."

"Kevin—" Tina began.

"That's a good idea," said Giles, interrupting her. "We would also like twenty packets of birdie treats please."

"You must have a lot of very hungry birds," said the pet shop owner nervously.

"Or one very large one," said Giles with a smile.

"Right," said the pet shop owner, hurrying off to fill the order.

Giles's parents were waiting for them outside in the car.

"I hope nobody saw us," muttered Mrs Barnes as they drove off. "They'll think we're all certifiable. Sixty-three pounds of bird seed . . ."

Back home, Giles organized the preparations for the big feed. With Tina and Kevin's help, he brought down all the bird cages from the attic and began dusting and cleaning them. They polished the metal bars until they shone. They made sure the perches and roosts were firmly attached. They even put fresh newspaper at the bottom of each cage.

"They're just ghosts," muttered Mrs Barnes. "Isn't this getting a little out of hand?"

"We have to do our best to show them we're sorry about what happened," Giles explained.

"I can't believe I'm doing this," said Tina. "It's so unscientific."

"Cheer up, Tina," said Kevin, "who knows, maybe it'll work."

When all the cages were cleaned, they started filling the plastic feeding trays with seed from the huge sacks. They filled all the water bottles from the kitchen tap. And, for good measure, they hung birdie treats from the bars of every cage. Giles had prepared a bird feast the likes of which had never been seen in the animal kingdom.

"Now," said Giles, "let's set them all up in my room. That's where Melanie Jones kept them."

It took them a good half hour to carry all the cages upstairs and arrange them. By the time they were done, Giles's bedroom was absolutely crammed, filled wall to wall with bird cages. There were cages on every shelf, cages across the desk, on the window sills, tall cages on pedestals standing side by side, cages on the bed and floor.

"If this works," said Mrs Barnes, "I hope I never see another bird again as long as I live."

Suddenly a ghost bird appeared inside one of the cages. It sat on the perch, looking out at Giles, then noticed the tray of bird seed. It hopped over to the feeder and started eating.

"Here we go!" Giles exclaimed.

Then they came fast and furious. The ghost birds materialized so quickly that Giles couldn't keep track. They were filling up all the cages in his room, sometimes two or even three birds to a cage. And they were ravenous, gobbling seed, slurping water, gnawing at birdie treats.

"They're eating everything!" Giles shouted.

Except eating wasn't exactly the right word. The birds ate and ate, but the piles of food weren't getting any smaller. Still, it didn't seem to bother the birds. Giles lost track of time as the feast went on. But then, one by one, the ghost birds started disappearing.

First a budgie flickered out of sight.

Then a cockatiel vanished into thin air.

Then three finches evaporated in a puff of ghostly smoke!

"It's working!" Giles called out.

"I should have brought my ghostometer," Tina said.

"We don't *need* the ghostometer!" said Giles. "Can't you see, it's working!"

The birds were blinking out like burned-out light-bulbs, faster and faster. As Giles watched, he felt a ghostly prickle move up his spine. He looked over his shoulder. The ghost of Melanie Jones had appeared amongst the cages.

"Look," Giles whispered, pointing.

"She's the one who interrupted my shower," mumbled Mrs Barnes.

The ghost of Melanie Jones didn't look sad anymore; she was smiling, nodding and smiling as she watched her birds eating the best and biggest meal ever. Then she began to fade, faint and silvery, until there was nothing left. After that the rest of the ghost birds vanished with little pops of light until all the cages in Giles's room were finally empty.

"You must be a genius!" Kevin said to Giles. "You've done it!"

"It was completely unscientific," said Tina in a shaky voice, "and yet it seems to have been successful."

"Not completely," said Mrs Barnes in a stern voice. "Look at this!"

The regal ghost parrot was perched on her shoulder.

"Hello, hello!" it said.

"No, look, it's fading, too!" said Giles.

"Good-bye, good-bye," said the parrot, and, with a little puff of light, it was gone.

"Well, that's a relief," said Mrs Barnes.

"You looked pretty good with a parrot," said Mr Barnes, hugging his wife.

"Well, they're all gone now," said Giles, gazing at the empty cages. Strangely, the house seemed too quiet, and he felt a twinge of sadness. He hadn't realized it, but he'd become rather fond of the birds, and all their noise and activity. The ghosts had kept him so busy he hadn't even had a chance to miss his old friends. In fact, he'd made some new ones. Maybe the summer wouldn't be so bad after all.

"What are we going to do with all that seed?" Mr Barnes said.

"And the cages?" said Mrs. Barnes.

"Maybe," Giles said with a smile, "we should get some birds."

Have you read all of the Barnes & the Brains adventures?

S0-AET-355

Hate Mail

OCT 0 2 2014

J FIC Polak

Polak, M.
Hate mail.

DISCARDED

PRICE: $9.95 (3559/he   )

Hate Mail

Monique Polak

Orca currents

ORCA BOOK PUBLISHERS

Copyright © 2014 Monique Polak

All rights reserved. No part of this publication may be reproduced
or transmitted in any form or by any means, electronic or mechanical, including
photocopying, recording or by any information storage and retrieval system now
known or to be invented, without permission in writing from the publisher.

Library and Archives Canada Cataloguing in Publication

Polak, Monique, author
Hate mail / Monique Polak.
(Orca currents)

Issued in print and electronic formats.
ISBN 978-1-4598-0776-1 (bound).—ISBN 978-1-4598-0775-4 (pbk.).—
ISBN 978-1-4598-0777-8 (pdf).—ISBN 978-1-4598-0778-5 (epub)

I. Title. II. Series: Orca currents
PS8631.O43H38 2014   jC813'.6   C2014-901563-1
C2014-901564-x

First published in the United States, 2014
Library of Congress Control Number: 2014935381

Summary: Jordie has a hard time going to school with his cousin with autism.

MIX
Paper from
responsible sources
FSC® C016245

*Orca Book Publishers is dedicated to preserving the environment and has
printed this book on Forest Stewardship Council® certified paper.*

Orca Book Publishers gratefully acknowledges the support for its
publishing programs provided by the following agencies: the Government
of Canada through the Canada Book Fund and the Canada Council for the Arts,
and the Province of British Columbia through the BC Arts Council
and the Book Publishing Tax Credit.

Cover photography by iStock
Author photo by Studio Iris Photography

ORCA BOOK PUBLISHERS
PO Box 5626, Stn. B
Victoria, BC Canada
V8R 6S4

ORCA BOOK PUBLISHERS
PO Box 468
Custer, WA USA
98240-0468

www.orcabook.com
Printed and bound in Canada.

17 16 15 14 • 4 3 2 1

For my friend David Riverin,
who loves to read

Chapter One

"Are we out of juice boxes?" I call out.

Mom walks into the kitchen. She's on the phone. I can tell from the way she keeps shaking her head she's upset. She must be talking to Aunt Anna. I bet they're talking about Todd.

Just before the school year started, Aunt Anna, Uncle Fred and my cousin Todd moved back to Montreal from a small town in upstate New York. We have more services for kids like Todd here, and Mom thought it would help Aunt Anna if they lived closer to us.

"Who would write something like that?" Mom says into the phone.

"Juice boxes?" I whisper.

She opens the cupboard under the sink, pulls out a packet of juice boxes and hands it to me.

"I hate orange," I mutter. But Mom isn't listening.

I toss a box of orange juice into my lunch bag. Maybe Tyrone will trade me.

Mom follows me to the front hallway. She tucks the phone between her ear and her shoulder so she can hear Aunt Anna while she kisses me goodbye. "Have a good day, Jordie," she calls out after me.

As Mom closes the door behind me, I can still hear her talking to Aunt Anna.

"What I don't understand is how anyone could be so deliberately cruel.

Not only to think those awful things, but to put them into a letter." There's a pause, and then she adds, "Thank goodness Todd doesn't know."

What letter? I wonder.

When I get to our locker, Tyrone is checking his cell phone—Tyrone is always playing with his phone. "What's good, bro?" he says, high-fiving me.

Samantha and Isobel walk by. They're both wearing tight striped T-shirts and short skirts. "Looking good, ladies!" Tyrone says, and they laugh. Samantha gives me a little wave.

I spot Todd coming down the hallway. I look away, pretending to search my locker.

The bell rings, and I slam the locker shut. The hallway is filling up with kids moving in every direction. Even if I wanted to, I couldn't see Todd now.

"Where's your babysitter?" I hear a guy call out.

I know without looking up that he must be talking to Todd. Correction: not talking to Todd. Talking at Todd. Except for the teachers and Darlene, Todd's aide, hardly anyone at school talks to Todd. Not even me.

"Aren't you a little old for a baby-sitter?" the same voice asks.

I don't hear Todd answer.

"Quit bugging him," a girl's voice says.

Then I hear a loud "*Oops!*" It's probably Todd.

When some kids start snickering, I know for sure it's him.

"Leave me alone!" He is shouting now. "Go away!" Up the hall, I see Todd is on his back on the floor, his arms flapping. Kids are backing away. When Todd loses his temper, he really loses it.

I feel bad for Todd, I swear I do. I know I should go over and help.

Except no one—not even Tyrone—knows that Todd is my cousin.

Where's Darlene anyhow? She gets paid to look after him.

As I'm thinking that, I spot the top of Darlene's head. Her curls make her look like a walking mop. "Todd! Are you hurt?" Darlene is one of those loud, slow talkers. It probably comes from spending her days shadowing kids like Todd.

I can't see Todd through the crowd of kids now, but I can hear his labored breathing as he picks himself up from the floor.

"Okay then," I hear Darlene say. "Up you go. It's a good thing you're not hurt. You're just a little dusty." She looks around at the kids still watching. "Did one of you push him?"

"I'm just a little dusty," I hear Todd say. If he was pushed, he doesn't tell Darlene.

I need to pass Todd and Darlene to get to history. I move as quickly as I can, elbowing my way past the other kids, hoping Todd won't notice me.

From the corner of my eye, I see the back of Todd's head. He has the same copper-colored hair as me. We got it from our moms. If I get too close to Todd, someone might figure out we are related. My life sure was less complicated before Todd turned up at my school.

Mr. Dartoni is at the whiteboard. "This morning," he says, "we're going to be looking at one of the most famous letters in Canadian history. It's a letter Louis Riel wrote to his followers. This letter was later used to convict Riel of treason."

It reminds me of the letter Mom and Aunt Anna were discussing on the phone. The cruel letter Todd is not supposed to know about.

Chapter Two

I try getting out of it. I tell Mom my English essay is due Tuesday and I haven't started yet.

Mom is pinching dead leaves off a houseplant. I can tell from the way she's concentrating—collecting leaf bits so they don't land on the carpet—that she isn't going to budge. "It's important to make time for family, Jordie," she says. "You'll write your essay tomorrow."

My dad is in the living room, reading the paper. "It'll be fun, bud," he adds without lifting his nose from the sports section.

It won't be fun, and we all know it.

We're going to the Pierre Elliott Trudeau Airport because Todd is obsessed with airplanes. Ask him how his day is going and Todd will start jabbering about wingspans, fuselage and vertical stabilizers.

It's part of Todd's condition, like going ballistic when he's angry and being unable to read other people's feelings. Most people can tell when someone's bored. A bored person yawns, looks out the window, checks the time. But even if you do all those things while Todd is talking about airplanes, he won't notice. He just keeps jabbering.

On our way to Aunt Anna's, I ask about the letter.

Mom and Dad exchange a look. "What letter?" Mom says.

"The one I heard you and Aunt Anna talking about. You used the word *cruel*. I figured it had something to do with Todd."

"I'd rather not discuss the letter," Mom says.

"Was it from school?"

"Jordie." Dad's voice is stern. "Your mother said she'd rather not discuss it."

Mom sighs. "And for god's sake, Jordie, please don't mention it in front of Todd. All I will tell you is that it's a disgusting letter—and it's about your cousin."

"You're kidding."

Dad sighs. "Why would your mother kid about something like that?"

Dad turns onto the street where Aunt Anna, Uncle Fred and Todd live.

Todd is pacing on the sidewalk outside the apartment.

"Be kind," Mom says.

"He's your cousin," Dad adds.

I slide open the back door of our van to let Todd in. "Hey, Todd."

It's as if he hasn't heard me. He doesn't say hi. He doesn't make eye contact. He just gets into the van, leaving this huge space between us. Then he starts bouncing in his seat. I get dizzy watching him bounce like that.

"Hi, Todd, honey," Mom says, flashing Todd a smile, which of course he doesn't notice. "How you doing?"

"We're going to the Pierre Elliot Trudeau Airport," Todd says. He's looking at his shoes.

As if we didn't know we were going to the airport!

Todd keeps bouncing. "The Dash 8 series was introduced in Canada in 1984."

The Dash 8 is Todd's favorite airplane. Thanks to our family visits to the airport, I'm getting to be kind of an expert in planes myself. "The Dash 8's the one with a twin engine, right?" I ask Todd.

"The Dash 8 is a twin engine turbo-prop," Todd says.

Mom pats Todd's hand. Just for a second, before he can object. Todd hates when people touch him, especially strangers. Mom is trying to help Todd work on that. "I hate to interrupt when you boys are bonding, but where's your mom and dad?" she asks.

Todd's bouncing again. "Inside."

Except for when he's babbling about airplanes, Todd uses really short sentences.

"I'll go get them," I offer. It's one way to get a break from Todd. He's not a bad kid, but, well, it's hard not being able to have a normal conversation.

I hear Aunt Anna and Uncle Fred coming downstairs. "I'll need to get footage in the arrivals area," Uncle Fred is saying. "Families meeting up after long absences. Guys holding bouquets and looking nervous."

"Can we discuss this later, Fred?" Aunt Anna sounds tired.

Uncle Fred jumps down the last two steps.

"Look who's here," he says when he sees me. "My favorite nephew."

"I'm your only nephew."

"Technicalities!" Uncle Fred ruffles my hair. "I was just telling your aunt about my idea for a documentary film."

A man walks into the lobby. He stops to look for something on the shelf near the mailboxes.

"Hi, George," Uncle Fred says to him.

George doesn't answer. He just mutters something about his newspaper. "That kid of yours didn't take it, did he?"

"Why would Todd take your news-paper?" Aunt Anna sounds annoyed.

"Well, I know he's got that…that…" George doesn't look at either Uncle Fred or Aunt Anna.

"Autism," Aunt Anna tells George. "Our son Todd has autism. I'm sure he didn't take your newspaper. In fact, I don't appreciate your making those kinds of remarks about Todd. You obviously don't know a thing about autism."

"We better go," I say quietly. I don't want Aunt Anna getting into a fight with this guy. Besides, Mom, Dad and Todd are waiting for us.

Uncle Fred doesn't seem to notice there's a problem. "Hey, George," he says, "when you have some time, I'd like to talk to you about this idea I have for a film…"

We park in the lot and then walk to the terminal. Mom and Aunt Anna are up ahead, followed by Dad and Uncle Fred. Uncle Fred is telling Dad about his idea.

Which leaves me with Todd.

I know I have to make an effort. Todd is my cousin.

"Think we might see a Dash 8?" I ask him.

"Do you mean the Bombardier Q400 turboprop?"

"I guess."

"The Dash 8 Bombardier Q400 turboprop arrives at 2:07 PM from Radisson. The Dash 8 Bombardier Q400 turboprop was released in 2000. It has the longest fuselage in the series."

"How do you know stuff like that?"

"Fuselage is the tube-shaped body of the plane."

"You memorized that, right?"

"Uh-huh," Todd says to his shoes.

"You don't think that's a little weird?"

"The Dash 8 Bombardier Q400 turboprop is more fuel efficient than the Dash 8 Bombardier Q200."

At the observation area, I don't have to worry about what to say to Todd. All he wants to do is watch airplanes. He presses his face against the glass when a jet taxis in our direction.

"The Boeing 777 has the biggest tires on any commercial jet," he says when the plane comes to a stop.

I like planes too. But after twenty minutes of watching them and listening to Todd rattle off specs, I'm done.

Todd doesn't notice when I walk away.

Mom, Dad, Aunt Anna and Uncle Fred are sitting on benches, sipping coffee from paper cups. Uncle Fred is talking about his documentary. Aunt Anna rolls her eyes.

"Hey, bud," Dad says to me. "Having fun?"

"Sure," I lie.

Mom looks over to where Todd is. "You shouldn't leave your cousin alone like that."

So much for getting a break from Airplane Man.

I'm heading back to do my cousinly duty when I feel a light tap on my shoulder.

Before I even turn around, I know it's Samantha. No one else smells that good.

"Jordie!" she says. "What are you doing here?"

"I just came to watch airplanes with my—" I stop mid-sentence.

Samantha looks at me and then over to the window where Todd is standing, his face pressed against the glass.

"—with my parents. That's them over there." I point to the benches.

"Samantha!" a woman's voice calls from down the corridor.

"I better go," Samantha says. "We're picking up my grandmother."

"Well, good to see you…" It's not easy making conversation with a girl who smells as good as Samantha.

"Have fun," Samantha says.

I'm watching her walk away, when she turns around and adds, "With your parents."

Chapter Three

"Mind if we sit here, ladies?" Tyrone says to Isobel and Samantha.

Today's assembly must have been scheduled on short notice because there are no chairs out. The girls make room for us on the floor.

I'm sitting so close to Samantha our elbows touch. I owe it all to Tyrone. I might get better grades, but when it comes to talking to girls, Tyrone is at the top of the class.

There's static as Mr. Delisle, our principal, adjusts the microphone.

The teachers are seated on two long benches at either side of the gym. They make shushing sounds to signal the assembly is about to begin. Todd and Darlene are sitting on one of the benches too, but as long as I look straight at Mr. Delisle, they are out of my range of vision.

"Good morning," Mr. Delisle says. "I want to begin by saying a few words about bullying. It's a topic you've already heard a lot about, but I like to think I have something fresh to add to the discussion."

Some kids make shuffling noises at the back of the room, and somewhere closer to me, someone is whispering. Mr. Delisle waits until the room is quiet.

"As I'm sure you've all observed, each one of us is different. We come in different shapes and sizes. We like different flavors of ice cream. My personal favorite is double fudge."

A few kids laugh when he says that. "We all have different abilities, and we face different challenges," Mr. Delisle continues.

I think about how good Tyrone is at talking to girls and how terrible Todd is at talking to anybody.

Mr. Delisle clears his throat. "A lot of people speak about the need for tolerance. How we have to tolerate those who are different from us. But I don't think tolerance is enough—not for our community here at Riverview High School."

"I want you all to consider the word *tolerance* for a moment." Mr. Delisle pauses. I try thinking about the word, but I'm distracted by Samantha's smell and the feeling of her elbow against mine.

"We tolerate things we don't especially like. We tolerate rainy days and bruised apples. Don't tell my wife if you meet her, but I tolerate my mother-in-law."

This time, everyone laughs.

"This year at Riverview, we're not just going to tolerate each other. We're going to aim for something better. *Acceptance*." Mr. Delisle looks around the room, his gaze taking in each of us and stopping for the briefest moment in the far corner, where Todd and Darlene are.

He picks up a sheet of paper from the podium. "A few more announcements before you return to your classes. I know you're eager to hear about this year's class trips. The grade elevens are going to Quebec City. Grade tens will visit the Biodome and the Insectarium. The grade eights and nines are going to a flying school. And grade sevens, you'll be attending this year's Blue Metropolis Literary Festival."

There is some excited whispering after that, but Mr. Delisle isn't finished. "I nearly forgot to tell you—I'm implementing a new policy: Saturday-morning detentions. Students who are rude to their teachers, who skip classes, who miss their regular detentions or who engage in any kind of bullying behavior can expect to spend their Saturday mornings here with me in this gym. Now I want to wish all of you a pleasant day. I expect you to give serious thought to the matters we've discussed this morning."

The teachers stand up from the benches and wait for us at the back of the gym.

When I get up, I see that Darlene and Todd are still sitting. They must be waiting for the rest of us to leave.

Todd scratches under both his arms over and over. If a typical person's armpits get itchy, he might scratch once or twice. But Todd keeps scratching as the gym empties. When autistic kids engage in repetitive behaviors like that, it's called *stimming*.

"What's that freak doing?" Tyrone whispers. I know he means Todd.

"How the hell should I know?"

Samantha and Isobel are right behind us. "That doesn't sound very accepting," Samantha tells Tyrone.

Tyrone doesn't like admitting he's wrong. "Maybe the kid's got fleas." At least he didn't call Todd a freak. Tyrone turns to me. "Do you think he's got fleas?"

I pretend not to hear.

Tyrone nudges my shoulder a little too hard. "Do you?"

Samantha saves me from having to answer. She sidles up next to me. "Did I ever tell you," she says, "that your hair's a cool color?"

"Uh, no, you never told me. But, uh, thanks. It's nice getting a compliment from a girl...I mean from you." I realize how dumb that sounds. Why can't I be as smooth as Tyrone?

But Samantha doesn't seem to mind. She lifts her chin toward where Todd and Darlene are sitting. "You know what's funny? Your hair's the same color as Todd's."

The good feeling I got when Samantha paid me that compliment?

It's gone.

Chapter Four

"Can't we walk over?" I ask Mom. "You're always saying we should walk more."

Making kids attend parent-teacher night is another one of Mr. Delisle's bright ideas. At least tomorrow is a professional-development day, so we can sleep in.

"I know. But I told your Aunt Anna we'd pick her and Todd up."

"They won't mind. C'mon, Mom. When's the last time we went for a walk?"

"Okay," Mom says. "Let me phone and see if they can get there on their own."

The leaves have started to fall from the trees, and the air has a new crispness. Soon it will be Halloween.

"I forgot how fast you walk." Mom's cheeks are flushed from keeping up with me.

I can't tell Mom I am desperate to get to parent-teacher night before Todd and Aunt Anna show up. If anyone spots Todd and me with our moms, they'll know we're related. Mom and Aunt Anna look more alike than Todd and I do.

Mr. Delisle is waiting inside the entrance, shaking parents' hands.

Two grade eleven students are handing out a map of the school.

"Don't forget to check out the bake sale in the gym," one of them says.

Mom cranes her neck looking for Aunt Anna and Todd. I wonder if Mom has always felt responsible for Aunt Anna, who is four years younger than she is, or if she only started worrying about her after Todd got diagnosed.

I tug on the sleeve of Mom's leather jacket. "We should go right upstairs. That way, we won't have so long to wait."

There are already people milling outside Room 221. Mrs. Turcot, my home-room teacher, has left the door open. She is sitting at her desk with a parent. A girl named Lisa, who's in my home-room, hovers by the classroom door.

"Five minutes alone with the parent, then she invites the kid in. The whole thing takes ten minutes...unless of course you've got ADD or something," Lisa explains when my mom and I join the line. "Don't forget the sign-up sheet." She points to a sheet behind the door.

There are four names ahead of ours. "Wanna sit?" I ask my mom. There's a row of chairs in the hallway.

Mom checks the time on her cell. "Maybe I'll go back downstairs and look for Anna. Make sure everything's okay."

"No problem," I tell Mom. "I'll hold our spot."

Tyrone hasn't turned up yet. Samantha is not here either.

I take a seat in one of the chairs. A group of parents are clustered nearby. I'm not trying to listen in on their conversation, but they're talking so loud, it's hard not to.

"Who ever heard of Saturday-morning detentions?" one mom says.

"I'm with you," a dad chimes in. "It's ridiculous."

"You know what's even more ridic-ulous?" another woman asks. Her voice is nasal. She lowers it before she goes on, but I can hear her. "Letting kids into this school who need all kinds of extra looking after."

I look up at the woman. She's got spiky blond hair, and she's wearing a black coat, with short black boots. "By the time kids get to high school, they should be able to manage without aides," she adds.

"And it's our tax dollars paying for those services!" a man mutters. "What worries me is that with so much money being spent on special-needs students, my kid won't get what he needs."

I know they're complaining about kids like Todd. If my mom were here, she'd say something.

I could say something.

Only I don't want anybody to know that Todd's my cousin.

By the time my mom gets back, our names are at the top of the list.

"Everything okay?" Mom asks. "You look a little off, Jordie."

"I'm fine. Did you find Aunt Anna?"

"Yup. I said we'd meet up with her and Todd later in the gym. At the bake sale. Someone mentioned chocolate cupcakes."

"Well, Jordie," Mrs. Turcot says when I sit down with her and Mom. Mrs. Turcot's mark book is open on her desk. "I've told your mom that overall you're a strong student. The only area that needs improvement is that sometimes you seem distracted."

"I'll try to work on that." I look Mrs. Turcot in the eye so she'll know I'm serious.

"My stomach feels kinda off," I tell Mom when our appointment is over. I put my hand on my belly. "I don't think a chocolate cupcake is a good idea right now."

"Do you feel like you're going to be sick?" Mom asks.

"Maybe."

Which is how I get out of going to the bake sale.

Mom gets Dad to pick us up. She makes him open all the windows in the van. She thinks the fresh air might make me feel better.

When we get home, Mom insists on holding my arm as I walk up the front stairs. I want her to think I'm still feeling queasy, so I stop on the third stair. Mom stops too.

Our eyes meet. I expect her to offer to make me tea or get me Pepto-Bismol. Instead, she gives me a sharp look and asks, "Jordie, have you told anyone at school that you and Todd are cousins?"

When I don't answer, Mom shakes her head. "There's something wrong with you, Jordie," she tells me, "and it's a lot worse than a stomachache."

Chapter Five

It's after ten when I wake up. The house is dead quiet.

I go down to the kitchen in just my boxers. If Mom were home, she'd make me put on a T-shirt. I leave the cereal box and my bowl, which still has milk in it, on the kitchen table. When I burp, I nearly apologize, but then I remember there's no one around to hear me.

Mom hasn't left a note. I turn on the TV, but there are only kids' shows and lame talk shows on. I should study for Mr. Dartoni's history quiz, but hey, I've got all day. I turn on the computer. I figure I'll message Tyrone, see what he's doing.

Maybe it's because I've got the quiz on my mind that my eyes land on the word *History* at the top of the screen.

When I click on *History*, I can tell right away Mom was the last one online. Who else would google spider plants and recipes for tofu teriyaki? I hope that isn't what we're having for supper. I scan the rest of the list. Mom's visited three websites about teens who have autism and a website about depression. The autism I get— Mom's trying to help Aunt Anna deal with Todd—but why is Mom looking up depression? We don't know anyone who's depressed, do we?

I'm about to click on the depression link when I notice the next item. It's Mom's Gmail account. I click on it.

A couple of seconds later, I am looking at Mom's inbox. I should tell her to make sure she logs out of her Gmail account when she's done. She doesn't want people reading her emails.

I should close this window, but I don't.

Instead, I scroll down the list of messages. She's got thousands. Hasn't Mom ever heard of Trash? Some of the messages are work related—people inquiring about Mom's houseplant watering service, her rates, whether there's a discount if they sign up for a year. But most of the messages are from Aunt Anna. They've got subject lines like *Having a really tough day, call me NOW!* and *Worried Sick About Fred.* Why is Aunt Anna worried about Uncle Fred? I'm about to click on that message when another one catches my eye. The subject line is only two words: *Hate Mail*.

I know even before I click on it that this must be the letter I heard Mom talking about on the phone. Most stuff you see on the Internet is typed out, so I'm expecting to see a typed-out letter.

What I don't expect to see is messy handwriting scrawled across a sheet of lined paper.

Aunt Anna must have scanned the letter. There's no date or greeting at the top; no *yours truly* at the end. It just starts.

I can't stand looking at that kid of yours. I'm sick of seeing him outside or in the schoolyard at Riverside, scratching under his arms and talking to himself like a lunatic.

Your kid's a freak.

I need to stop and take a breath after I read that. Sure, I think Todd is weird, and just last week Tyrone called him a freak. But seeing the word written out like that seems worse.

I don't know why you even let that kid out of the house.

You should keep him locked up so regular people don't have to look at him.

Or put him in a zoo where freaks like him belong.

The words are so mean, so angry, I can't keep reading.

I shut down the computer. My eyes are stinging. I turn the TV back on. A woman in heavy makeup is talking about a diet. "After a few days, you won't even miss sugar," she says, smiling into the camera. I hit the Power button on the remote to make her go away.

I go upstairs to get my history folder. It was wrong of me to open Mom's email. I should forget I ever saw that letter. Erase it from my mind the way

Mr. Dartoni erases the whiteboard at the end of class.

Except I can't.

The words I read keep coming back to me. *Your kid's a freak. Put him in a zoo where freaks like him belong.*

How could anyone think those things about Todd? I'm halfway up the stairs when I turn back. I re-open the computer and go back into Mom's email. The end of the letter is even worse than the beginning.

If you ask me, you should put that freak down, put him out of his misery. Just like you'd put down a sick animal. That freak of yours doesn't deserve to live.

I didn't really have a stomachache last night, but I've got one now. Even after I vomit into the toilet, my stomach still hurts.

Chapter Six

"I'm going to have to confiscate that gun," the security guard tells me.

"It's plastic," I tell him. "It's part of my costume. I'm a gangster."

But he insists. It's only when he's patting me down, checking for knives or alcohol, that I realize it's Mr. Delisle dressed up like a security guard.

"That's a very convincing costume, Mr. De—"

Mr. Delisle presses a finger to his lips. "What are you trying to do, blow my cover?"

I adjust my sleeves as I walk into the gym. I'm wearing my dad's black suit—Mom pinned up the pants, but the sleeves on the jacket are still too long—a black shirt and red tie. It's hard to believe this is the gym where we play basketball and floor hockey and have assemblies.

There are platforms for dancing and another one for the DJ. Paper skeletons hang from the ceiling, and there are jack-o'-lanterns on the table where a student council kid is selling soda and chips.

"I love your costume!" I hear some girl squeal. When I look to see who she's talking to, I know right away it's Tyrone. Who else would dress up like a rapper? He's wearing a velour tracksuit, with thick gold chains and a giant pair of headphones around his neck.

There are two girls with him. I can tell from her silver dress and pink hair that one is supposed to be a groupie. The other girl is wearing a black wig and a navy skirt and jacket. She must be some kind of businesswoman.

I make my way over. It's only when I get closer that I realize the girls are Isobel and Samantha.

Tyrone has one arm around Isobel's waist. I can't help feeling a little jealous when he wraps his other arm around Samantha.

"We're his dates," Isobel chirps. She even sounds like a groupie.

"You are? I didn't know we were supposed to have dates. How come you didn't tell me, Tyrone?"

Tyrone lets go of Samantha so he can smack the side of my head with the back of his hand. When he opens his mouth, I see the gold grill over his teeth. "It must've slipped my mind. But hey, you're welcome to hang with us. If the ladies don't mind."

"Of course we don't mind," Samantha says, which makes me feel better about the whole date thing.

"If you don't mind my asking," I say to Samantha, "what are you supposed to be?"

"Tyrone wanted us both to dress up as groupies, but I refused. I'm his producer."

"You look hot in that wig." Even before the words are out of my mouth, I realize how dumb they sound. "I mean you look...well, you know...good. Extremely good."

Samantha doesn't seem offended. "You look good too," she says. "Even if you're not really the gangster type. I like to think I'm the producer type."

"Totally," I say, which makes Samantha smile.

Tyrone and Isobel are first on the dance floor. When he presses up close against her, Mr. Dartoni, who is dressed like a priest, walks over and taps Tyrone's shoulder. "Not so close," he says.

I'm trying to figure out how to ask Samantha to dance. I don't think Tyrone asked Isobel; he just swept her onto the dance floor. I don't think I could do that with Samantha. *Do you want to dance?* Nah, too dorky. Plus, what if she says no?

I'm trying to come up with the right words when Samantha grabs my hand. "What are you doing?" I ask her.

"I was waiting for you to ask me to dance," she says. "But I ran out of patience."

The DJ is playing Eminem's "Same Song & Dance." Samantha sways to the beat. I nod when Eminem sings, "I like the way you move." Tyrone and Isobel are dancing next to us. Tyrone winks at me.

While we dance, Samantha and I comment on the other kids' costumes. "That's so original," she says about some guy dressed like a box of Chiclets. She also likes the girl in the mummy costume, her entire body wrapped in white medical gauze.

I don't think anything about it when a guy in a pilot's uniform passes the platform where we're dancing. I only see the back of him: shiny black cap, white shirt with gold epaulets, gray pants.

Samantha nudges me. "I don't see Kool-Aid. Do you?"

"I don't see Kool-Aid either, just 7-Up and Coke. You thirsty? You want to get something to drink?"

"I said, 'I don't see his aide.'" Samantha shouts so I can hear her over the music. She lifts her eyes in the pilot's direction. How could I not have known it was Todd? Then again, I didn't expect him to show up at a school dance.

"His aide must be here somewhere. His parents wouldn't let him come to a dance unsupervised. They'd have hired Darl—" I stop myself. I don't want to sound like I know too much about Todd.

"Oh, there she is!" Samantha says. Now I see Darlene too. She's in line at the refreshments table. She's dressed as a unicorn, with her horn wrapped in tin foil. Maybe it's her way of saying it's good to be different.

I don't know where Todd is. The lighting is dim, making it hard to see. Why am I worrying about him anyway? That's Darlene's job.

A guy from homeroom is dressed like a hockey puck. "That's a cool costume," I say to Samantha, but her back is turned to me now, and she's dancing with Isobel.

I don't understand girls.

Since I'm not one of those people who enjoys dancing alone, I step off the platform, hoping no one is watching me.

I'd buy a soda, but I don't want to get stuck talking to Darlene—or Todd.

I go stand by the wall. Isobel and Samantha are still dancing. I wonder where Tyrone is. When I get tired of standing around, I take a bathroom break.

Even before I walk into the bathroom, I can hear laughter. What's going on in there?

Tyrone is sitting on a chair blocking one of the stalls. He moves his head to the beat of the music he is listening to.

The laughter comes from Mark, one of Tyrone's buddies, who is wearing a Spider-Man costume. "If you were a real rapper," Mark tells Tyrone, "you wouldn't be listening to music in some bathroom. I'm getting outta here. Why don't you just leave whoever's inside there alone? I'll wait for you outside."

That's when I realize someone is trapped inside the stall.

Whoever it is has started banging like crazy on the stall door.

Tyrone has this big dumb smile on his face.

The guy inside bangs harder. He's going to hurt himself if he keeps that up.

It's not nice to tease some kid the way Tyrone is doing, but I have to admit it's kind of funny to hear the guy freaking out.

Now he's trying to crawl out from underneath the stall door.

Tyrone laughs as he swats at the guy's hands.

The guy starts howling. It's this weird high-pitched nervous howl. Only one person howls like that.

Todd.

"Let him out!" I tell Tyrone.

Mark bangs on the bathroom door then pushes it open. "Security's coming!" he hisses.

Tyrone pulls the chair out of the way. "Okay," he says, "whoever you are, joke's over. You can come out now." But Todd is howling so loud he can't hear Tyrone.

If Todd knew I was here, it might help him calm down. But there's no way I want Tyrone to know Todd and I are related.

Mr. Delisle bursts into the bathroom. Todd is still blubbering. He won't come out of the stall. I see Mr. Delisle's eyes land on the chair behind Tyrone. I know he's piecing together what has happened.

Darlene is outside, shouting, "Are you in there, Todd? Todd, are you all right?"

Mr. Delisle walks over to the stall door. "Todd," he says, "it's me, Mr. Delisle. I'm sorry for what's happened.

I'm going to ask the others to leave. When you're ready, you can come out. Darlene is waiting for you outside the bathroom. Are you okay with that, Todd?"

The blubbering lets up and Todd says, "Okay."

Mr. Delisle curls his finger to indicate he wants to talk to me and Tyrone outside. We follow him to the corridor. Mr. Delisle's dark eyes look even darker than usual.

"It was just a joke. I swear I wouldn't have done it if I'd known it was him inside," Tyrone tries telling Mr. Delisle.

"I had nothing to do with it," I add. "I just walked in and..."

Mr. Delisle waves the back of his hand in the air as if Tyrone and I are mosquitoes he would like to swat.

Mark is running down the hall with Isobel and Samantha. Mr. Delisle calls them over. "Saturday-morning detentions," he says in a voice I've never heard him use before, "for every one of you!"

"We didn't do anything," Isobel says. "We were just talking to Mark."

"I'll see all of you at eight AM sharp on Saturday," Mr. Delisle says.

Then Mr. Delisle turns to Darlene. "I'll need to speak with you and Todd later. But you can let him know he's got a detention too—for not telling you he was leaving the gym."

"You can't go giving out detentions like that," Mark says. "You're a security guard!"

Tyrone nudges Mark. "That's no security guard, doofus," he says. "That's Mr. Delisle."

Chapter Seven

When I see the lights on in the living room, I think my parents must be watching late-night TV.

But the TV isn't on. Dad is in his armchair. Mom is on the couch across from him. They're speaking in low voices, but the conversation stops when I walk in. That's how I know they're waiting for me.

Do they know about the detention?

"Did you have fun?" Mom asks.

"Dance with any good-looking girls?" Dad wants to know.

"Yes and yes." I'm thinking that if they heard about the detention, they would have mentioned it. "It's pretty late. I better get to bed."

Mom uncrosses her legs. "We wanted to have a word with you."

"Now?"

Mom nods. She looks so serious that for a moment I think they do know about the detention.

"It wasn't my fault."

"What are you talking about, Jordie?" Dad asks.

I need to change the subject—fast. "What exactly do you want to talk to me about?" I don't sit down. That way I might still be able to get away.

Dad must know what I'm thinking. He gestures toward the empty spot on the couch. "Have a seat."

I plop down. Mom moves in a little closer. "We want to talk to you about your cousin. About Todd."

"I know his name."

"Jordie, don't be rude to your mom."

"Sorry, Mom." I don't look at her when I apologize.

"We know it isn't easy for you." Dad doesn't say what *it* is, but I figure he means having Todd for a cousin.

"When I was your age," Mom adds, "all I cared about was wearing the same brand of jeans as the other girls."

"What do girls' jeans have to do with anything?" I ask.

I half expect Dad to tell me I'm being rude again, but he doesn't. "What your mom means is that when you're a teen-ager, you put a lot of stock in what other kids think of you. Too much stock."

"You can't keep hiding the fact that you and Todd are related." Mom sighs after she's said that. Dad sighs too.

"Having a cousin who's a fr—" I stop myself. But I can tell Mom and Dad know what I was about to say. "—who's autistic is a lot harder than not having the right pair of jeans."

"It's a lot harder for Todd than it is for you," Mom snaps.

I try to explain. "I guess I worry if the other kids know Todd and I are related, they'll look at me differently. They'll laugh at me."

"Laugh at you? For having a cousin who has autism? Why, that's ridiculous!" Mom says.

"I think we need to go at this from another angle," Dad says. "Todd needs your support. He looks up to you, Jordie. He's proud to be your cousin."

"Proud? Proud's a feeling. Todd doesn't have feelings!" I don't mean to raise my voice.

"Jordie, we've been over this a hundred times. Of course Todd has feelings,"

Mom says. "It's just hard for people with autism to express their feelings."

"Look, I don't know why we've got to have this conversation right now." I get up from the couch and start heading upstairs.

"Your Aunt Anna's having a hard time," Dad says to my back.

I turn to look at him and Mom. "Is that supposed to be some kind of newsflash? I know Aunt Anna's having a hard time. Mom spends half of every friggin' day on the phone with Aunt Anna talking about it." I'm raising my voice again.

"It isn't only Todd she's worried about..." Mom says quietly.

I'm only half listening. Maybe because I'm too ticked off. It's only when I'm putting on my pajamas that I think about what Mom just said. By then, Mom and Dad are upstairs too. I hear them in the bathroom, brushing their teeth.

I open my bedroom door and call out, "What else is Aunt Anna worried about?"

The brushing sounds stop and then Dad says, "Maybe it's better if we talk about it in the morning."

I need to brush my teeth too. They're both still there when I get to the bathroom. Mom's putting on face cream. Dad's flossing.

"So what's wrong with Aunt Anna?"

Mom and Dad exchange a look in the mirror.

"It's Uncle Fred," Mom says.

"He's depressed," Dad adds.

"Uncle Fred—depressed? What are you talking about? He was in a great mood when we went to the airport."

Mom and Dad exchange another look. They're deciding how much to tell me.

Mom replaces the lid on her jar of cream. "When we went to the airport, he was in one of his up phases. Now he's in a down phase."

"Everyone has ups and downs," I say.

Mom sighs. "What your Uncle Fred has is different. We're pretty sure he has something called manic depression. He's had it before."

"He has? How come I never heard about it?"

"You were little the last time it happened," Mom says. "It was just after Todd was diagnosed."

I don't say what I'm thinking—that if I was a dad and my kid got diagnosed with autism, I'd be depressed too.

Chapter Eight

If Mom and Dad sleep in, I should be able to slip out to Saturday-morning detention without telling them about it. Or at least without telling them about it in person. They'll need to sign a form, but I'll worry about that later.

I tiptoe downstairs and try not to crunch when I eat my cereal. Because I know they'll wonder where I've gone, I leave a note on the kitchen table.

Dear Mom and Dad,

Since you were already kind of upset last night, I didn't think it was a good time to tell you I got a Saturday morning detention. Honestly, I didn't do anything wrong. It was a case of being in the wrong place at the wrong time. Detention's over at 12:30. I'll come straight home. Your son, Jordie.

I'm crossing out the *Your son* part (they know I'm their son) when the phone rings. I spring up from my stool to grab the portable, but the damage is done. Mom has picked up the phone in her bedroom. "Anna," I hear Mom say, her voice still groggy, "is it Todd? Or Fred?"

I put my bowl in the dishwasher and grab my jacket.

I slip out the front door and take a deep breath. That was a close call.

Better that I'm not around when Mom finds out about the detention.

I break into a jog. Moving feels good. I'm not looking forward to spending four and a half hours staring at the gym walls, but at least Samantha will be there.

I hardly notice when a van pulls up at the Stop sign. Not until the passenger window rolls down, and I see my mom behind the wheel. In her penguin pajamas! I turn around to make sure no one's watching.

"Mom, you can't drive around in your pajamas!"

"Get in the van, Jordie!" I can tell from her voice she means business.

"I think it's better if I walk. I can use the exercise. Look, I'm sorry I didn't tell you about the detention."

"That's not all you didn't tell me about, Jordie. In the van! Now!" I get in.

"Why didn't you tell me Todd got a detention too?"

"I figured you'd find out. Are you planning to drop me off at school? Maybe you could leave me at the corner. No offense, but I don't want anyone knowing my mom drives around town in penguin pajamas."

I think maybe that will make Mom laugh, but it has the opposite effect. "You know what your problem is, Jordie? You care way too much about what other people think!"

I don't say anything after that, and neither does Mom. She drives right up to the front entrance. Tyrone is coming from the other direction. I try not to care when he walks up to my mom's door. "Good morning," he says. "Nice pj's!"

I'm getting out of the van when my mom puts her hand on my elbow. "Jordie, like it or not, you're going to have to keep an eye on your cousin today."

I turn around to face her. "What about Darlene?"

"Mr. Delisle asked Darlene to come in, but she wasn't available. He couldn't find a replacement. So you're it." There's no point in arguing.

There's a row of desks at the front of the gym. Samantha, Isobel and Mark are already there.

Mr. Delisle comes in after us. He is wearing plaid shirt and jeans. Seeing him dressed like that is almost as weird as seeing him in a security guard costume. "Have any of you seen Todd?" he asks. "What about you, Jordie?"

"Nope, I haven't seen him." I try to keep my voice casual. I'm willing Mr. Delisle not to tell the others that Todd is my cousin.

Mr. Delisle gives me an odd look. "Well then, Jordie," he says, "could you wait by the front entrance and bring Todd to the gym once he arrives?"

When I get to the front entrance, Aunt Anna is there, helping Todd take off his coat. She waves when she sees me. "You'll look out for him, won't you, Jordie?" she asks me.

"Uh-huh," I tell her. "Okay, Todd." I gesture for him to follow me. I know he'll get upset if I take his arm. "We're going to the gym."

Todd's eyes are fixed on the floor. "I got a detention," he says. "I didn't tell Darlene I was going to the bathroom. And then the door wouldn't open. That made me mad."

"You won't let anyone tease him, will you?" Aunt Anna whispers to me.

I follow Todd down the hallway. What would it be like, I wonder, to have a normal cousin? Someone to hang out with, play video games, listen to music, talk about girls. Sometimes, it sucks to be me.

When we get to the gym, the others aren't at their desks. They are by the bleachers, huddled around Mr. Delisle.

Mr. Delisle waves when we come in. "Over here!" he calls out.

I go stand between Tyrone and Samantha. Todd stays a few feet back from the rest of us.

"I don't see much point in having you people sit around twiddling your thumbs for four and a half hours," Mr. Delisle says. "I'm sure you'd prefer to do something useful. So you're going to spend the morning cleaning up the schoolyard."

"Isn't child labor illegal?" Tyrone asks.

"Nothing illegal about it," Mr. Delisle tells Tyrone. "Not if the tasks contribute to youngsters' education, health, physical and moral development. And I promise you—they will." Why am I not surprised he knows all about child labor laws?

"I wish you'd told us we'd be working outside," Isobel says to Mr. Delisle. "I wouldn't have worn a skirt."

Chapter Nine

I have to give Mr. Delisle credit. He could make us do all the work, but he's raking leaves too. His face is shiny with sweat. The seven of us are stuffing leaves into giant compostable paper bags. The wind is blustery, and we have to hold on to the paper bags so they don't fly away. I pull my tuque down over my forehead.

Mark hasn't got a hat. He looks different without gel in his hair. "Isn't this the janitor's job?" he grumbles.

Mr. Delisle leans on his rake. "You complaining, Mark?"

"No, sir. Just asking."

"Hey, there's a leaf in your hair," Tyrone tells Isobel. He pulls the leaf out and hands it to her. Isobel giggles. Only Tyrone could find a way to turn detention into a way to impress girls.

Todd isn't saying anything, which is better, I guess, than babbling about Dash 8s. He isn't working as quickly as the rest of us. Maybe it's because every time he scoops another bunch of leaves into his bag, he tamps them down.

"Hey, Mr. D, if we get these leaves cleaned up before twelve thirty, you gonna let us go home early?" Tyrone asks.

Mr. Delisle puts down his rake and uses both hands to massage his lower back. "Did I mention the leaves in the side yard? There are twice as many there as there are here."

Tyrone groans.

"Do you think I can leave the six of you to your own devices for a few minutes?" Mr. Delisle asks. "I need to go inside and get some aspirin."

"We'll be fine," Tyrone answers for all of us.

"Good," Mr. Delisle says, "because I'd hate to have to give you all another Saturday detention. Mind you, the boiler room could use a scrub."

Once Mr. Delisle is out of sight, Mark and Tyrone stop scooping leaves. Tyrone pulls his cell out of his pocket and checks for new messages. Mark is watching Todd. "Hey, buddy," he tells him, "it'd go a lot faster if you waited to do that till your bag was full."

Mark's tone is friendly, but Todd isn't any better at recognizing a person's tone than he is at reading body language. He doesn't say anything.

"Did you hear me?" This time, Mark's tone is less friendly.

Todd still doesn't respond.

"Well, did you?"

"Uh-huh," Todd finally answers. Only he's still tamping down the leaves.

I think about the promise I made to my mom and Aunt Anna. I take a deep breath. "Maybe you should leave Todd alone," I tell Mark. "We've all got our own way of doing stuff. Doing things in a certain order makes him feel better."

Samantha, who is crouched on the ground near me, gives me a smile. The cool air has made her cheeks red.

Mark lifts his chin in my direction. "What are you? Some kind of expert on freaks?"

My heart is thumping in my chest. I know Samantha is listening, and that makes me want to do the right thing.

"Todd's not a freak. He has autism. Lots of people have it." I know this would be a perfect moment to say that Todd's my cousin, but I don't.

I can't.

Just then, the back door of the school swings open and Mr. Delisle comes out. Mark and Tyrone start shoveling leaves into their bags again.

"It's recess time," Mr. Delisle call out. "I brought you a little snack."

"He's not a bad guy," Isobel says, "for a principal."

Mr. Delisle has granola bars. They're not the store-bought kind we're used to. "My wife made them," he explains, handing them out. "They're wheat-free. She wants me to cut back on gluten."

Mr. Delisle doesn't rake as quickly as he did before. I catch Mark looking over Todd's shoulder a couple of times. I don't understand why it bugs Mark so much that Todd keeps tamping down the leaves in his bag. I'd say something, but I'm afraid Mark will start ragging on me again.

I'm lugging bags to the compost bin when I notice Mark hunched over Todd. Now what's going on?

I rush over. Mark is showing Todd how to fill his bag more quickly. "Like this," he's saying as he shoves leaves into the bag.

Mr. Delisle has come over too. "Leave Todd alone," he tells Mark.

"I'm just trying to help him." Mark claps Todd's back. Mark doesn't know Todd hates to be touched.

It is a simple gesture—Mark meant to show he didn't mean any harm—but it sets Todd off.

"Don't touch me!" Todd wails so loudly that if anyone in the neighborhood is trying to sleep in, they are awake now.

Mark backs away, but Todd keeps wailing. "Don't touch me! I told you not to touch me! Stop! I said stop!"

Only, the person who can't stop is Todd.

"Let's give Todd some space," Mr. Delisle says. He looks worried. He's used to having Darlene around to help with Todd. Mr. Delisle drops his voice. "Everything's going to be okay, son," he tells Todd.

Samantha is next to me. "Aren't you going to help?" she asks.

I go over to Todd. I don't touch him. I try talking the way I've heard Aunt Anna and Mom talk to him—in a low, soothing voice.

"It's me—Jordie." I'm talking so quietly I'm sure the others can't hear me. "I'm here. No one's going to hurt you, Todd."

Mr. Delisle has stepped away to give us some privacy. "The rest of you," I hear him tell the others, "back to work."

It takes Todd a while to settle down, but he does.

When I'm back to stuffing leaves into a bag, Mark nudges me. "I didn't know you were so good with freaks," he whispers.

"Quit calling him a freak!" I whisper back.

Samantha is close enough to overhear our conversation. I smile at her, expecting her to smile back. She must be impressed I stood up for Todd.

But she just shakes her head.

"Is something wrong?" I ask her.

Samantha shakes her head again. "I don't know why you can't admit you two are related."

Chapter Ten

I'm not the kind of kid who listens in on other people's phone conversations.

What happens is I'm in the kitchen, about to call Tyrone, when I pick up the portable and hear Mom and Aunt Anna talking.

I could say "Oops" and hang up, but, well, I don't.

They are discussing the letter. Aunt Anna doesn't use the word *letter* though. She uses the words *hate mail*.

"The police say it's a hate crime, but that there isn't much they can do about it. That's why I'm going public. You can't keep telling me not to, Julie. I've had it with pretending everything's okay. There are horrible people out there, people who hate kids like my son. I want to expose that hatred." Aunt Anna is sobbing.

"Oh, Anna," Mom says and I can practically see her wringing her hands, "I know how hard this is for you. But you need to think about Todd—about what's best for him. He's a shy child. If you go to the media, there will be interviews."

I'm picturing it in my head, Todd's face in the newspaper and on TV, his voice on the radio. It would be a total disaster! And what if people see Aunt Anna and they figure out she's mom's sister and I'm Todd's cousin? Then what?

"They won't want to talk to only you, Anna," Mom continues. "They'll want to talk to Todd. And what if he finds out about what's in the letter? Frankly, I don't think he could handle it." Mom pauses. "Even a normal child would find it difficult."

Yikes, I think to myself, that's the worst possible thing to say to Aunt Anna.

"*A normal child*? My god, Julie! I can't believe you just said that! How many times have I told you children with autism are not *abnormal*?" I'm surprised at how quickly Aunt Anna switches from sad to angry.

"I'm so sorry, Anna. Of course, I know you're right. The word just slipped out, I think because I'm so ups—"

Aunt Anna won't let her finish. "I know you try to be a good sister and a good aunt, but sometimes I think you don't understand what my life is like!

Between looking after Todd and worrying about Fred!"

"I'm trying to understand, Anna, honestly I am. I know how tough things are. I'm trying to be supportive. Why do you think I encouraged you to move back here? But maybe with so much pressure…you're not thinking clearly."

Aunt Anna makes a noise that sounds like a growl. "For your information, I am thinking perfectly clearly. And let me tell you something else: just because you're my big sister doesn't mean you're always right. You always try to smooth things over, but you know what, Julie? Sometimes it's better to stand up. Even if it's hard!"

When Aunt Anna says that, I remember what happened at detention. I tried standing up for Todd, and Aunt Anna is right, it was hard.

Mom won't back down. "This isn't about you, Anna. It's about Todd and what's best for him. I know you're upset, but you have to put your son first."

"Don't speak to me like that," Aunt Anna hisses. "I have always put Todd first. Always. You know that!"

"Anna, can you at least agree not to do anything rash? Can we talk about this in a few days when we've both calmed down?"

"All right," Aunt Anna says, "I'll wait a few days. But I'm warning you, Julie, if I still feel like this, I'm going ahead with my plan."

Mom sighs into the phone. "I think a few days will give you some perspective. By the way, have you talked to Fred about it?"

"Fred?" Aunt Anna laughs. It's not a happy laugh. It's an I-can't-take-much-more kind of laugh.

"Yes," Mom says, "how does Fred feel about your plan to go public with the letter?"

"Fred?" Aunt Anna says again. I wonder if maybe Aunt Anna is cracking up too. "Fred can't talk about anything except that ridiculous movie he wants to make. He hasn't slept in two weeks. He's up writing treatments and proposals."

"Oh no." Mom sounds almost as distressed as when Aunt Anna was talking about the hate letter.

Neither of them says anything for a moment. Then Mom adds, "The not sleeping. Isn't that what happened last time?" Mom pauses. "Before he crashed?"

Chapter Eleven

Mom is usually out watering plants when I get home from school Tuesdays. So when I see the van in the driveway and Mom in the front window with her jacket on, I know something's wrong.

"I need your help," she says when I come in.

"What for?"

"We've got to get right over to Anna's. It's an emergency."

"Have you ever noticed," I say, when we're in the van, "how it's always an emergency with Aunt Anna?"

Mom doesn't stop for a yellow light. "You know what I've noticed, Jordie?" she says. "That you're only interested in your own well-being."

"Ouch," I say. "That hurt."

But is it true?

When we reach the third floor where Aunt Anna lives, one of their neighbors is taking his trash out. It's the same guy who was unfriendly to Aunt Anna the other day.

He doesn't seem to mind talking to my mom. "You her sister?" he asks when he sees us at Aunt Anna's door. "You look the same."

"Yes, we're sisters."

The man gives me the once over. "So you're his cousin?"

"Uh-huh." I don't feel like getting into a conversation with this guy.

"Good thing you're not autistic too," the man says as he walks off. His voice drops when he says the word *autistic*, as if he's afraid that by saying it too loud, he might catch it.

Mom's back stiffens. "You shouldn't talk that way about my nephew—or about anyone else," she says, but the guy is out of earshot.

Mom rings, but no one answers. The door is unlocked, so we walk in. Todd is sitting on the living room rug, hunched over the latest issue of *Aviation Week*.

"Todd, honey, we're here," Mom says.

Todd is muttering to himself, probably reading from the magazine.

Mom goes over to him. "I know this must be very stressful for you, Todd," she says.

This time, Todd grunts.

Because anything beats hanging out with Todd, I follow Mom into Aunt Anna and Uncle Fred's bedroom. The curtains are drawn and the lights are off. Aunt Anna is perched on the edge of the bed. Uncle Fred is lying down, though it's hard to know for sure it's him because the sheets are pulled over his head. The room smells like old gym socks.

Mom flicks on the light switch.

"No!" Uncle Fred moans from underneath the sheets.

Mom turns off the light.

"Has he eaten?" Mom asks Aunt Anna.

"Not a thing."

Mom walks over to the side of the bed. "Fred," she says, addressing the sheets, "you've got to see a doctor. We're worried about you."

Uncle Fred doesn't say anything. The sheets move up and down as he breathes.

"Fred," Mom continues, "Anna and I are going to take you to the hospital. We need you to get up now. Anna"— she pats my aunt's shoulder—"you'll need to pack him some clothes and his toothbrush."

"I'm not going," Uncle Fred says from underneath the sheets.

"Oh yes you are." I recognize my Mom's no-nonsense voice. I feel like telling Uncle Fred there's no point arguing with her. "If you don't go with us now, Jordie's going to phone an ambulance."

I am?

I can hear Aunt Anna rustling in the bathroom.

Mom kneels down. She whispers— I guess she doesn't want Aunt Anna to hear—"Fred, if they have to drag you out of here in an ambulance, it's going to be hard on Todd. It's a lot easier on him if you come with us now."

At first, Uncle Fred does not respond. But then he throws off the sheet that is covering his head and says, "All right. I'll go."

Aunt Anna is watching from the doorway. "Thank god," she says.

Mom helps Uncle Fred up. She even has to help him lace his shoes.

"What do you want me to do?" I ask her.

"You can look after Todd. We're taking Uncle Fred to emergency at Montreal General. If it's a long wait, you may be here all night, Jordie."

"You're kidding."

I try to distract Todd when Mom and Aunt Anna lead Uncle Fred out of the apartment. "Wanna show me that magazine?" I ask him. "Any Dash 8s in there?"

But my strategy fails. Todd lumbers over to the door, clutching the magazine under his arm. "Where's Dad going?" he wants to know.

This could be the first time I've ever heard Todd start a conversation that wasn't about airplanes. Todd is worried—the way any kid would worry about his dad.

Uncle Fred looks confused, and Mom and Aunt Anna are too busy steering Uncle Fred out the door to answer Todd. I figure it's up to me. "Your dad has to see the doctor. We're going to hang out."

"Hang out?"

"Yeah, me and you. Do stuff. Like cousins do," I tell him.

"Okay, we're going to hang out. Like cousins." Todd's voice is flat, but I get the feeling he's pleased.

I remember what Mom said in the van—how I'm only interested in my own well-being. So I try to think about Todd's well-being. About what would make him feel better right now. "Wanna show me your magazine collection?"

Todd keeps his magazines underneath his desk. "I have fifty-seven issues," he says. "Two are doubles. So it's really fifty-six."

I grab a magazine from the pile and start flipping through it.

Todd scratches under his arms. He keeps scratching. I know it's that stimming thing he does. Part of me wants to tell him to stop, but the nicer part of me knows I shouldn't.

I remember something Mom once told me: neurotypical people—that's the scientific term for people who do not have disorders like autism—engage in repetitive behaviors too.

"Ever notice how your dad is always playing with the remote?" she had asked me. Dad must have heard us talking because he called out from the other room, "Or how your mom is always pinching dead leaves off plants?"

Now Todd is straightening out the pile of magazines.

"All I did was grab the one on top," I tell him.

Todd looks down at the floor. "I like the edges lined up," he says.

"Why?"

Todd doesn't have an answer. Now that he's got the edges of his magazines lined up, he starts scratching at his pits again.

I need to do something to distract him. "I guess you're looking forward to visiting that flight school."

"Yeah."

Well, I think, that wasn't exactly a conversation starter. I need to come up with something better. "How many seats in a Dash 8?"

"The Dash 8-300 or the Dash 8-100?" Todd actually looks at me for a second.

"Uh, both, I guess."

"The Dash 8-300 has fifty seats. The 100 has thirty-seven seats. I also know their cruising altitudes."

"You do?" I try to sound interested.

"The Dash 8-300 and the Dash 8-100 have the same cruising altitude: twenty-five thousand feet."

"I'm sorry about your dad."

Todd's Adam's apple jiggles in his throat. Is it possible I am about to have a normal conversation with Todd, the kind of conversation regular cousins have? Is Todd going to say he's worried about his dad? And when he does, will I be able to say something helpful?

But when Todd speaks again, he doesn't mention Uncle Fred. "Twenty-five thousand feet," he says, "is seven thousand, six hundred and twenty meters."

Maybe Todd catches me looking at him funny. Or maybe he's worried about his dad. Because now Todd keeps repeating, "Twenty-five thousand feet is seven thousand, six hundred and twenty meters." He says it over and over, faster and faster like a top spinning round. "Twenty-five thousand feet is seven thousand, six…"

Todd pays no attention when I ask him quietly to stop.

In the end, I have no choice but to shout. "Stop it! Stop it now! You're driving me crazy!"

Todd stops.

Then he does something even worse.

He starts to cry. I've never seen anyone sob so hard.

Watching him is awful.

"Your dad's going to be okay," I tell him. "He's just going through a hard time."

Todd wipes the snot from his nose with the back of his hand.

"Don't hug me," he says when he finally calms down.

Chapter Twelve

I wonder if Aunt Anna had anything to do with choosing the destination for this field trip. She meets a lot with Mr. Delisle, so maybe it was her idea that the grade eights and nines visit a flight school. She must have known it would make Todd happy.

We take a bus to the school, which is in Lachute, a town in the foothills of the Laurentian Mountains. Todd and Darlene sit up front. But even from the back, where I sit with Tyrone, Mark and the girls, I can see Todd stimming. I don't know if it's because he's anxious (Uncle Fred has been in the hospital for over a week), or if he's excited about spending a day around airplanes.

"Do a lot of girls take flying lessons?" Isobel asks Mr. Gendron, the owner of the flying school and our tour guide for the day.

"More than half our clients are men," Mr. Gendron tells her, "but women make excellent pilots. Are you thinking of becoming a pilot?"

"Now I am!" Isobel says.

"Have you ever seen a crash?" Mark wants to know.

"Never," Mr. Gendron says. "We have a perfect safety record. When a plane crashes, it makes the news. But there are far more car accidents than plane crashes."

Our tour begins in a two-story office building. There's a snack bar on the main floor. Everyone laughs when Tyrone asks the woman standing behind the counter if she serves airplane food. "You know the kind that comes in plastic trays with foil wrapping?"

Mr. Gendron takes us upstairs to show us two classrooms and the dispatch office. That's where students book flights and pick up documents and keys.

"Every plane has its own logbook," Mr. Gendron says as he pulls out a logbook from the shelf and opens it. "Pilots and student pilots record their information after every flight. We also record all maintenance and service to the aircrafts."

Most kids wander down the hallway to look through the giant windows into the hangar, but not Todd. He's studying the logbook the way I would study for one of Mr. Dartoni's quizzes.

Darlene is standing by the wall, supervising from there.

I tense up when I see Mr. Gendron clap Todd on the shoulder. But Todd doesn't freak out. Maybe he is too absorbed in the logbook to notice. "You seem to be an extremely focused young man," Mr. Gendron tells Todd. "Maybe you should consider a career in aviation."

Todd doesn't react. But Darlene grins. "Oh, wouldn't that be wonderful?" she says.

The coolest thing upstairs is the flight simulator. Mr. Gendron explains how this machine—it's basically an armchair with a giant panel in front— teaches pilots how to fly in complete darkness. "See that part of the screen?" he says, pointing to a blacked-out area on the screen. That's what zero visibility looks like."

"I'd freak out," Samantha says.

"Not if you studied instrument flying," Mr. Gendron tells her. "Another thing I should explain is that pilots must constantly monitor weather conditions. You may have noticed the computer outside the dispatch office. Before every flight, our instructors and students check the weather. Weather is a tricky thing," he adds, gesturing to a window at the back of the room. "Today is a perfect example. It's bright and sunny, but by this afternoon, we're supposed to get record high winds. I can tell you that none of my planes will be in the air this afternoon. The good news for you people is that means you'll be able to visit one or two of the teaching planes on the ground."

"I really want to go inside a Cessna 172," Todd says.

Mr. Gendron looks impressed. "It's not often I meet someone your age who knows about airplanes."

I see a couple of kids nudge each other and I'm expecting someone— maybe Tyrone or Mark—to make a crack about Todd, but no one does.

When I hear a weird retching sound from the back of the room, my first thought is that someone must be airsick. My second thought is that doesn't make any sense since we aren't in the air.

Everyone else notices too. Darlene's hand is over her mouth and her eyes look like they might pop out of her head. It's clear to all of us that she is about to be sick.

"I think she needs a barf bag!" Tyrone calls out.

This time, no one laughs at Tyrone's joke.

Darlene rushes to the bathroom. When she comes out, she is so weak she can barely speak. She thinks it's food poisoning. Her husband is coming to get her. "Your mom is going to have to pick you up," she tells Todd, "or there won't be anyone to watch you."

When Todd's face crumbles, I know I have to do something.

"I'll watch out for Todd."

"You will?" Darlene and Tyrone say at the same time.

I can feel Samantha's eyes on my face.

I take a deep breath, and then I say, "I will." I pause for a second. Then I force myself to look right at Tyrone. "Look," I say, "there's something I never told you. Todd's my cousin."

Tyrone's mouth falls open. "No way," he says.

Mr. Gendron brings Darlene downstairs. Samantha goes to get her a glass of water. Darlene takes small sips.

Darlene taps my arm when I pass her. "Are you sure you can manage?" she asks.

"Sure I'm sure." I hope I sound more confident that I feel.

Chapter Thirteen

"He's your cousin?" Tyrone says. We've been inside the Cessna 172 (we took turns sitting in the pilot's seat). Now Mr. Gendron has gone back inside, and a few of us are walking along a runway. The wind is so strong we have to keep our faces down.

Mark nudges Tyrone. "I can't believe

you didn't figure that one out. Couldn't you tell from the hair?"

Todd is behind me.

"Yup," I say, "we're cousins." I try to make it sound like it's no big deal.

"How come you never said anything?" Tyrone asks me.

"Just because."

A brochure Isobel picked up at the dispatch office flies out of her hand. Tyrone tries catching it, but the wind sweeps up the brochure and sends it hurtling down the runway.

This sure is some crazy wind. It's whipping at our coats and howling in our ears. Another giant gust and the runway lights go out.

"Oh my god," Isobel squeals, "black out!"

We huddle closer. Tyrone puts his arm around Isobel.

Suddenly, there's a loud crack,

and a long thick branch comes flying at us. "Watch out!" Tyrone yells. Only it's too late. The branch whacks the side of Samantha's face.

"Are you okay?"

She can't hear me over the wind.

Samantha isn't okay. The right side of her face is already swollen. Now I make out an ugly gash on her cheek. It's bleeding. Samantha touches her cheek. She moans when she feels the blood.

I take off one of my mitts. Samantha winces when I press it against her face to stop the bleeding. "We need to get her back to the main building," I tell the others.

Only the wind is pushing us in the opposite direction.

"Who's got a cell?" Isobel has to shout so we can hear her.

Tyrone whips out his cell. He looks at the screen and then shakes the phone.

"Stupid thing isn't working. Maybe the wind blew out the cell tower."

"We can't just stand here," I say.

"Where are we supposed to go?" Tyrone shouts.

"We can go in there," Todd says.

We all turn to look at him. The others are as surprised as I am that Todd has said something.

"Go in where?" Tyrone asks Todd.

Todd gestures toward an airplane parked in front of us on the runway. "In there."

"It'll be locked," Tyrone says.

Todd shakes his head. "If there's a crash, people need to be able to open the doors from outside."

The little plane is only a couple of hundred feet away, but because of the wind, it takes us a while to reach it. Todd's right about the doors. They aren't locked. We pile inside.

Isobel finds a first-aid kit. There's antibiotic cream and gauze inside.

Samantha grimaces when Isobel applies the cream.

I'm the one who notices the blood in Samantha's right eye. Then Isobel sees it too. "Oh my god, Sam," she says. "Your eye—it's bleeding!"

"We need to get her to a doctor," I say.

"What are you planning to do—phone nine-one-one?" Tyrone asks. "'Cause there's no cell service."

"Does it hurt?" Isobel asks Samantha.

"Not really." Samantha squeezes her right eye shut and then opens it again. "I can't see from that eye," she says quietly.

Which is when Isobel starts screaming.

Todd tenses up. I can't blame him. The piercing sound of Isobel's scream fills the small plane.

Now Todd presses his hands over his ears and starts making this awful sound I've never heard before. It's like a horse whinnying. If it was anybody else, I'd put my hand on his shoulder to calm him down. But I can't touch Todd.

At least this makes Isobel stop screaming.

"Todd," I say as calmly as I can, "Isobel didn't mean to scare you. She's worried. Samantha needs a doctor, and the phone's not working." I can feel the others watching us. "Let's take a few deep breaths." I've seen Aunt Anna do this with Todd.

Todd and I breathe in and out. We do it a few times.

Todd drops his hands back to his sides and sighs. "If there's no phone," he says, "we can use the ELT."

"The ELT? What's an ELT?" I ask him.

"The emergency locator transmitter," Todd says. "Every plane has one. On a small plane like this it's usually in the cargo compartment."

The ELT is exactly where Todd said it would be. "Have you ever used one of these before?" Tyrone asks Todd.

"No," Todd says, "but I've read about them. An ELT gets activated automatically during a crash. There's a manual option too."

Ten minutes later, Mr. Gendron pulls up in the aviation-school truck. By the time we get to the hangar, the ambulance is already waiting for Samantha.

Chapter Fourteen

Todd sleeps over. Mom is impressed when I offer to sleep on the couch so he can have my bed. "He's a hero," I say, shrugging my shoulders.

"Thank goodness he knew about that ELT," Mom says.

"I'm a hero," Todd says when I go upstairs for a pillow.

"That's for sure," I tell him.

Todd talks to himself before he falls asleep. Even from the living room, I hear him repeating over and over, "I'm a hero. That's for sure." I think about going upstairs and complaining. But it probably wouldn't help. So I put the pillow over my head and fall asleep.

Aunt Anna has spent the night at the hospital with Uncle Fred. This morning, he is being transferred to the psychiatric ward. "It's the best place for him now," Mom explains over breakfast.

Todd observes his Wheaties floating in the milk.

"We'll drop by the hospital this morning. Does that sound okay, Todd?" Mom asks.

"Okay," Todd says without looking up.

Todd and I wait outside the gift shop when Mom goes in to buy a magazine for Aunt Anna. Todd shifts from one foot to the other. He doesn't look at me when he speaks. "It's my fault Dad's sad. Because I have autism."

"That's the dumbest thing I've ever heard," I tell him.

We have to get buzzed into the psychiatric ward. Uncle Fred's room feels like a prison cell. Aunt Anna sits on the bed, holding Uncle Fred's hand. Uncle Fred is snoring lightly, but he stirs when we come in.

He opens his eyes and looks at Todd, but Uncle Fred is too tired—or maybe too drugged—to speak. His face is stubbly, and he's wearing a green hospital gown. I want my old uncle back, the one who calls me his favorite nephew. If it's hard for me, what must this be like for Todd?

When I turn my head, I'm not surprised to see that Todd is scratching under his arms.

If stimming worked for me, I'd do it right now too.

"Fred, did you hear that Todd's a hero?" Mom says this extra loud, as if she thinks that by raising her voice, Uncle Fred might snap out of his depression. "He helped get a girl medical attention. There was a windstorm. The kids were visiting an aviation school."

Uncle Fred tries propping himself up. In a voice not much louder than a whisper, he tells Todd, "I'm proud of you, son." And then, as if saying that has taken all the energy he had, Uncle Fred slumps back down.

Mom and Aunt Anna are talking in the hallway. "I'll need to prepare Todd," I hear Aunt Anna say.

At first, I think they're talking about how long Uncle Fred will be in the hospital, only then Mom adds, "You don't want him finding out from the newspaper."

They're not talking about Uncle Fred.

They're talking about the letter. Aunt Anna must have decided to go public with it after all.

Uncle Fred needs his rest, and Aunt Anna wants to go home to shower. Mom agrees to drop Todd and me at the Children's Hospital so we can visit Samantha. She'll pick us up after she's taken Aunt Anna home.

Aunt Anna and Todd sit in the back of the van. I feel sick to my stomach when Aunt Anna starts talking about the hate letter. Why couldn't she wait to do that until the two of them are alone? Then I realize maybe she wants Mom's support—and mine too.

"Todd, honey," Aunt Anna begins, "you know what your dad said—about being proud of you? I'm proud of you too. Not just for helping that girl, but for being you. Look, there's something important we need to discuss." She waits for Todd to respond, but when he doesn't, she continues. "Someone really ignorant wrote a cruel letter—a hateful letter—about you and about people with autism. I wasn't going to tell you, but I've changed my mind. Because you know what, Todd?" Aunt Anna's voice breaks, "You keep demonstrating how smart and brave you are. I think we need to go public with the letter. Not just for you. For other kids with autism."

Mom bites her lip. "Todd," she says as she watches him in the rearview mirror, "you need to tell your mom if you're not comfortable with this."

"Your Aunt Julie is right. Are you okay with me sending a copy of the letter to the newspaper?"

Todd doesn't say yes or no. He just repeats something Aunt Anna said before, "A hateful letter about people with autism."

Mom sucks in her breath. "I'm still not sure it's the right thing to do, Anna."

"It's a pretty bad letter," I say.

"How do you know?" Mom and Aunt Anna ask at the same time.

"I...uh...I saw it. On the computer."

"You were reading my email?" Mom asks.

"It just kinda happened. You really need a lesson about Internet safety."

"That's not what this is about, Jordie."

Aunt Anna interrupts. "If Jordie's read the letter, he'll be able to support Todd if it goes public."

"That's right. I will." I have to say that. It's the only way to end the argument.

Even with a patch over one eye, Samantha looks good. We find her sitting in the lounge at the Children's Hospital. Her dad is with her. "I've got a vitreous hemorrhage," Samantha says. "Sitting up helps the blood vessels drain to the bottom of my eye. The good news is I'm not blind."

"Phew," I say.

Maybe it's because of the patch that Samantha doesn't notice right away that Todd's behind me.

"Todd!" she says when she sees him. She starts getting up from her chair, but her dad stops her.

"Samantha! The doctor said absolutely no bouncing around for at least twenty-four hours! Are you Todd?"

Samantha doesn't listen to her dad. She goes over to Todd—and kisses him.

Todd squirms and then wipes at his cheek. Not surprisingly, he's stimming again.

I sure wish Samantha would kiss me like that. I wonder if Samantha knows what I'm thinking—because I get the feeling she's trying not to laugh. "Hey, Jordie," she says, "I need to thank you too."

"Thank me? For what?"

"For having such a cool cousin."

Samantha's dad reaches out to shake Todd's hand, but I stop him. "Todd doesn't like when people touch him. Especially people he's not used to."

"I see," Samantha's dad says. "Well, young man, we're very grateful for what you did."

A woman with blond spiky hair is walking toward us. I'm almost sure it's the woman I heard bad-mouthing kids like Todd at parent-teacher night.

"Are you guys having a party without me?" Now I recognize the nasal voice.

"Todd, Jordie," Samantha says, "I don't think you've met my stepmom."

"Oh my god," Samantha's stepmom puts her hand over her mouth when she sees Todd. "You're the kid who saved Samantha? I didn't realize it was you."

Chapter Fifteen

We're having a family meeting at Aunt
Anna's. We ordered in cheese pizza—
it's the only kind Todd likes. Mom and I
are sitting on one side of the table. Aunt
Anna and Todd are across from us.

Aunt Anna's hands shake when she
starts talking about the letter. "I don't think
you need to read it, honey," she tells Todd.
Her eyes are already filled with tears.

"I don't need to read it," Todd says.

"But I think you need to understand a little more," Aunt Anna continues. "About the sorts of things that are in it."

Mom shakes her head. Aunt Anna leans closer to Todd. I'm facing him. This is going to be torture.

"The person who wrote it doesn't know anything about autism," Aunt Anna says. "The letter is full of misconceptions and prejudice. It says people with autism are...that they..." Aunt Anna is getting really choked up now.

Mom reaches across the table to pat Aunt Anna's hand.

Todd swallows a couple of times. He scratches under his armpits, but only once. "Some people think I'm a freak," he says. His voice is flat, but his lower lip is trembling.

I can't take much more of this. "Maybe we shouldn't focus on the letter," I say quietly. "Maybe we should focus on a plan of action instead. A plan Todd's okay with."

"I just want to be sure that Todd understands," Mom says. "Like your mom said," she adds, looking at Todd, "the letter is full of misconceptions and prejudice. There are people who don't know much about autism. And people are afraid of what they don't know. So they lash out by saying—or writing—cruel things."

"I'm not a freak," Todd whispers.

"Of course you're not," I tell him.

"But someone wrote that," Todd says.

Mom's eyes flash. "Someone ignorant and cruel wrote that," she says.

"Someone cowardly," Aunt Anna adds. "That's why they didn't sign their name."

Todd does something unusual now: he looks at me. I can tell he expects me to say something.

"I don't think you're a freak." And because I don't know what else to say,

I add, "Samantha definitely doesn't think so."

Todd thinks about that for a minute. "I helped save Samantha," he says. "Samantha understands about autism. A lot of people don't."

"You're right," Aunt Anna says. "That's why I want to tell the newspaper about this hate mail."

"Okay," Todd says. "Tell the newspaper."

The story makes the front page of *The Gazette*. There's a picture of Aunt Anna holding the letter. Todd is in the picture too, but he's in the background, reading one of his aviation magazines, and his face is fuzzy. The hate letter is on page three of the paper.

None of us expected that the article—and the letter—would go viral. By the time I get home from school the day after the article was in the paper, it's all over Facebook and Twitter. There are a couple of nasty comments, but most are sympathetic. "What can we do to help Todd and kids like him?" one of them asks.

Uncle Fred has been complaining about the hospital food, so Todd and I bring him a cheeseburger and fries. The nurse who's giving Uncle Fred his pills smiles when she sees Todd. "I noticed the last name on your dad's chart," she says. "You're Todd, right?"

Todd is looking at the floor. "I guess you read the article."

"I saw it on Facebook. It's an honor to meet you," the nurse says. "You're a brave guy."

"He takes after his old man," Uncle Fred says.

It's the first joke Uncle Fred has made in nearly three weeks. I decide it's a sign that he's going to make a full recovery.

Chapter Sixteen

"I think Samantha's hot," Todd says.

"Hotter than a Dash 8?" I ask.

We are sitting at the donut shop where Samantha works. She sent me a text asking us to meet her here. The air smells sweet and lemony, and I now understand why Samantha always smells so delicious. Her good smell isn't perfume, it's donuts.

Samantha is behind the counter, serving customers. Todd and I munch on our lemon-filled donuts while we wait for her to get her break.

A guy in a long wool coat walks by and taps his knuckles on our table. Todd bristles. It's that weird guy who lives on his floor. "You know what I heard?" the man says. He sure doesn't have very good social skills.

"Uh, hello." I hope that'll give him the message.

It doesn't.

"I heard some people say that letter is a hoax. They said you people made it up to get attention. But I told them you wouldn't do that. I said I was sure it was a real letter."

"It's a real letter," Todd says.

Before he shuffles off to his own table, the man looks back at Todd and says, "Listen, kid, I'm sorry if I've been unfriendly. I guess I didn't know much about autism."

Samantha catches the end of the conversation. "Hey," she says to the man, "there's gonna be a rally on Saturday morning to raise awareness about autism. We're meeting in front of Riverview High School at ten. You should totally come!"

The man can't resist Samantha's charm any more than Todd or I can. "Ten?" he says. Then he reaches into his pocket, takes out his agenda and a small pencil, and makes a note about the rally.

Todd is shredding his napkin into tiny pieces. I bet he's nervous about the rally. There could be a lot of new people there, and they might get closer to him than he's comfortable with.

"How does it feel to be a hero?" Samantha asks him when she sits down.

"Good. I guess."

"I was thinking," I say to both of them, "maybe Todd won't like being right in the middle of the rally. Maybe we can find a way for him to participate— but still give him his space."

Todd has made a neat pile out of the bits of shredded napkin. "I like to have my space," he says.

"Well then, we'll make sure you get plenty of space," Samantha tells Todd.

That is when I realize Samantha is not just being nice—she really likes Todd and appreciates his quirkiness. I should be happy for Todd, but instead I feel jealous. "So, do you get to eat all the donuts you want?" I ask Samantha, hoping to get her attention back on me.

"To be honest, I'm sick of donuts." Samantha has a pink scar on her cheek where the branch hit her, but her eye looks normal.

"So what'd you want to talk to us about?" I ask her.

"I got you guys something," Samantha says.

"Is it donuts?" Todd asks.

When Samantha cracks up, I start feeling jealous again. "It's way better than donuts. Close your eyes, okay? Both of you."

We close our eyes. I can hear Samantha running to the back of the donut shop. When she comes back, she is out of breath. "Okay," she says, "you can open your eyes."

Samantha hands me and Todd a beautifully wrapped package. "It's something you can work on together," she says.

Todd and I tear off the wrapping. Samantha has bought us a kit to build a model Cessna 172. "Wow," I say, "what a great present. It's got four hundred pieces. And it comes with a pilot and four passengers." I know it's Samantha's way of telling us she'll never forget that day at the flight school.

Todd is inspecting the box.

"Do you like it?" Samantha asks him.

Todd puts the box down and starts rearranging the napkin bits. "The Cessna 172 is okay. But the Dash 8 is still my favorite," he says.

I figure any minute now Samantha is going to run out of patience with Todd and realize I am a far better guy for her than my cousin.

But Samantha is not upset. "You know what I like best about you, Todd?" she asks.

Now Todd is scratching his pits.

"I like your honesty." Samantha reaches across the table. For a second, I think she is going to take Todd's hand, but instead she reaches for the model kit. "How 'bout on Saturday, after the rally, we go to the hobby store and see if we can exchange this for a Dash 8 kit?"

As if things weren't bad enough, now Todd and Samantha are going to be hanging out together after the rally.

I am trying to think of how I can fix things. Only I don't have to. Because Todd has a question.

"Can Jordie come too?" he wants to know.

Chapter Seventeen

It's too bad Uncle Fred can't be at the rally. At least he's sleeping and eating again. Mom thinks it's a combination of the new meds and his sessions with the psychiatrist. It turns out the psychiatrist is a documentary-film buff—so I guess she and Uncle Fred have lots to talk about.

A crowd has formed in the school-yard. Many people are carrying placards that say things like *Down With Hate Mail* and *Autism Is Not a Disease—Ignorance Is*.

As I'm stepping out of the van, Todd hands me a folded-up piece of paper, which I slip into my pocket. "You sure?" I ask him.

"Uh-huh," he says.

Now I notice the banner over the front entrance of the school. *Todd's Our Hero*.

Todd is going to stay in the van with Mom, Dad and Aunt Anna. Dad has unrolled the windows so Todd can be part of the rally and apart from it at the same time. I catch Dad's eye and point to the banner, so he'll be sure Todd sees it too.

A few kids who spot Todd through the open window start chanting his name. *Todd! Todd! Todd!*

When I look back at Todd, I see he's got his hands over his ears.

"Hey," I call out to the crowd in my loudest voice. "No chanting, okay?"

Mr. Delisle comes over to where I am standing. That must be his wife with him. I hope no one mentions what he said at the assembly about his mother-in-law!

Mr. Delisle addresses the crowd. "Ladies and gentlemen, boys and girls," he says, "now that Todd and his family have arrived, this rally can officially begin. Our guest of honor prefers to be part of the procession from inside the van. The rest of us are going to be walking to city hall to raise awareness about autism."

Teachers, kids and even the guy from Todd's building have come out for the rally.

I give Todd a thumbs-up before I join the crowd.

For a second, Todd looks puzzled, but then he gives me a thumbs-up back.

Darlene is there too. She's walking with a group of Riverside teachers.

Dad is driving the van slowly to the right of the crowd. When the van stops for a light, some kids start pressing in on it. They want to see Todd—and talk to him. "One at a time," I call out.

Tyrone apologizes for what happened at the Halloween dance. Mark is going to Florida at Christmas, and he wants to know what Todd thinks of Air Canada's Boeing 767.

"The 767-300 ER?" Todd asks.

"Uh, I guess," Mark says.

"The 767-300 ER was Boeing's first wide-body twinjet," Todd says.

Mark whistles.

At the next light, Mark's sister wants to meet Todd. She's reaching into the van, when I stop her. "Todd doesn't like when people he doesn't know get too close," I explain.

Samantha pushes her way through the crowd to join me. "Can you believe all these people?" she says. "And they're all here for Todd!"

As we approach city hall, Mr. Delisle and his wife come to march next to us. "Jordie," Mr. Delisle says, "I'm going to say a few words when we get there. I understand you've agreed to say something too."

"Yup," I say. "That's the plan."

Mr. Delisle explains a little about autism and how there are more and more students with autism in the public school system. Then he tells everyone about what happened at the flight school and how Todd was a hero. Mr. Delisle also gives his speech about acceptance.

Then it's my turn.

"I just want to say thanks to all of you for turning up today to show your support."

When I realize I've been talking to my feet, I look up. That's when I notice a blond-haired woman walking over to join the crowd. Samantha's stepmom.

I reach into my pocket. "Todd wrote a letter he wants me to read for him."

The crowd gets so quiet I can hear the sound of people around me breathing. I unfold the letter. In a weird way, I feel like Todd when I start reading it. As if we're one person. "Hello," the letter begins.

"A lot of things are hard for people like me who have autism. Such as making eye contact and hearing loud noises and being part of a crowd. That's why I asked my cousin Jordie to read this letter for me.

"I heard about the hate mail. A lot of people want to know who wrote it. But not me. Because, in a way, that letter did something good. It let me find out that you think I'm okay. That you don't think I'm a freak."

131

My voice breaks a little when I read that part.

"I want to say thank you to all of you for coming out today. I also want you to know that people with autism can do anything we want to do. Even if it's hard for us. And if you really want to help people like me, this is what you can do. You can treat us like we're human beings. You can ask us to do stuff with you."

People are clapping now, but I can tell they're trying not to make too much noise—they're clapping gently.

I clear my throat to let the crowd know there's still another paragraph left in Todd's letter. "I want to say an extra thanks to my mom, my dad, Aunt Julie and Uncle Lou. And especially to my best friend"—I clear my throat again; I really hope no one knows how close I am to crying—"Jordie."

Acknowledgments

Hate Mail is the result of a project called *Libres comme l'art*. Made possible by the Blue Metropolis Literary Foundation, the Conférence régionale des élus de Montréal (CREM), and the Conseil des Arts de Montréal (CAM), *Libres comme l'art* allowed me to be writer-in-residence at Riverdale High School in Pierrefonds, Quebec, during the 2013–14 school year. Together with Karen Scott's grade-nine English class, we brainstormed ideas for this novel. The students heard almost every chapter as I was writing it. They laughed at the right spots and groaned or raised their hands when things needed fixing. I am grateful to Ms. Scott's students: Saba-Lou Ahmad Khan, Megan Amofa, Tyrelle Anasara-Diab, Shane Jermie Antoine, Hamzah Bashir Ahmad, Matthew Boucher, Ali Chaudhry,

Kelly Cooperberg, Mae-Ann Dilidili-Sales, Kayla D'Ovidio, Rupert Jr. Edwards, Christian Ehninger, Fahad Elsabawi, Alicia Frederick, Cassidy Freidman, Shayne Gallagher, Devontay Green, Sabrina Hilton-Cuillerier, Sarah Joly, Awaiz Junjua, Christopher Kelly, Darlens Leveque, Jared Logan, Liam-Marshall MacLellan, Bhahee Shan Manoranjan, Brett Marineau, Georgia Pournaras, Amanda Powell, Jordana Schmits, John Skalkogiannis, Vito Tarantino and Kiara West-Philippeaux. A special thanks to Hamzah, who, during our first session, mentioned a hate letter targeting an autistic child that had recently made the news. Special thanks also to Ms. Scott for sharing her students; to student teacher Christina Christopoulos; to Principal Roger Rampersad for his enthusiastic support; to librarian Susan Strano for opening up her library for the project;

and to Suzanne Nesbitt of the Lester B. Pearson School Board for bringing the project to Riverdale. I'm also grateful to the terrific team at Blue Metropolis, in particular its president, William St-Hilaire, for her wise and energetic leadership; Florence Allegrini, who got things started; and Laure Colin, who oversaw every step of the way. Thanks also to Frédérique Bélair-Bonnet of CREM and Réjane Bougé of CAM. Thanks to Craig Quinn for talking to me about airplanes, and to Philippe Gélinas for inviting me to visit Dorval Aviation School. Thanks also to my friend Elizabeth Arnot for reading an early draft and providing invaluable feedback. Finally, thanks to the super team at Orca, especially to my editor, Melanie Jeffs, for her astute and sensitive comments.

Monique Polak has written several books in the Orca Currents series, including *Pyro* and *121 Express*, an ALA Popular Paperbacks selection. Monique lives in Montreal, Quebec. For more information, visit www.moniquepolak.com.